Archaeology: A Very Short Introduction

'Few introductory volumes on archaeology have covered the entire scope of the field in as lively and entertaining a fashion as this short book.'

Charles C. Boyd, *American Antiquity*

'a series of acute and entertaining short essays on the subject's great themes . . . this is a model of good writing for a general audience . . . [The] chapters rattle along, packed with information but never getting bogged down in too much detail . . . The book is full of jokes, but its serious message – that archaeology can be a rich and fascinating subject – it gets across with more panache than any other book I know.'

Simon Denison, Editor of *British Archaeology*

VERY SHORT INTRODUCTIONS are for anyone wanting a stimulating and accessible way in to a new subject. They are written by experts, and have been published in more than 25 languages worldwide.

The series began in 1995, and now represents a wide variety of topics in history, philosophy, religion, science, and the humanities. Over the next few years it will grow to a library of around 200 volumes – a Very Short Introduction to everything from ancient Egypt and Indian philosophy to conceptual art and cosmology.

Very Short Introductions available now:

ANCIENT PHILOSOPHY Julia Annas
THE ANGLO-SAXON AGE John Blair
ANIMAL RIGHTS David DeGrazia
ARCHAEOLOGY Paul Bahn
ARCHITECTURE Andrew Ballantyne
ARISTOTLE Jonathan Barnes
ART HISTORY Dana Arnold
ART THEORY Cynthia Freeland
THE HISTORY OF ASTRONOMY Michael Hoskin
ATHEISM Julian Baggini
AUGUSTINE Henry Chadwick
BARTHES Jonathan Culler
THE BIBLE John Riches
BRITISH POLITICS Anthony Wright
BUDDHA Michael Carrithers
BUDDHISM Damien Keown
CAPITALISM James Fulcher
THE CELTS Barry Cunliffe
CHOICE THEORY Michael Allingham
CHRISTIAN ART Beth Williamson
CLASSICS Mary Beard and John Henderson
CLAUSEWITZ Michael Howard
THE COLD WAR Robert McMahon
CONTINENTAL PHILOSOPHY Simon Critchley
COSMOLOGY Peter Coles
CRYPTOGRAPHY Fred Piper and Sean Murphy
DADA AND SURREALISM David Hopkins
DARWIN Jonathan Howard
DEMOCRACY Bernard Crick
DESCARTES Tom Sorell
DRUGS Leslie Iversen
THE EARTH Martin Redfern
EGYPTIAN MYTHOLOGY Geraldine Pinch
EIGHTEENTH-CENTURY BRITAIN Paul Langford
THE ELEMENTS Philip Ball
EMOTION Dylan Evans
EMPIRE Stephen Howe
ENGELS Terrell Carver
ETHICS Simon Blackburn
THE EUROPEAN UNION John Pinder
EVOLUTION Brian and Deborah Charlesworth
FASCISM Kevin Passmore
THE FRENCH REVOLUTION William Doyle
FREUD Anthony Storr
GALILEO Stillman Drake
GANDHI Bhikhu Parekh

GLOBALIZATION Manfred Steger
HEGEL Peter Singer
HEIDEGGER Michael Inwood
HINDUISM Kim Knott
HISTORY John H. Arnold
HOBBES Richard Tuck
HUME A. J. Ayer
IDEOLOGY Michael Freeden
INDIAN PHILOSOPHY Sue Hamilton
INTELLIGENCE Ian J. Deary
ISLAM Malise Ruthven
JUDAISM Norman Solomon
JUNG Anthony Stevens
KANT Roger Scruton
KIERKEGAARD Patrick Gardiner
THE KORAN Michael Cook
LINGUISTICS Peter Matthews
LITERARY THEORY Jonathan Culler
LOCKE John Dunn
LOGIC Graham Priest
MACHIAVELLI Quentin Skinner
MARX Peter Singer
MATHEMATICS Timothy Gowers
MEDIEVAL BRITAIN John Gillingham and Ralph A. Griffiths
MODERN IRELAND Senia Pašeta
MOLECULES Philip Ball
MUSIC Nicholas Cook
NIETZSCHE Michael Tanner
NINETEENTH-CENTURY BRITAIN Christopher Harvie and H. C. G. Matthew
NORTHERN IRELAND Marc Mulholland
PAUL E. P. Sanders
PHILOSOPHY Edward Craig
PHILOSOPHY OF SCIENCE Samir Okasha
PLATO Julia Annas
POLITICS Kenneth Minogue
POSTCOLONIALISM Robert Young
POSTMODERNISM Christopher Butler
POSTSTRUCTURALISM Catherine Belsey
PREHISTORY Chris Gosden
PRESOCRATIC PHILOSOPHY Catherine Osborne
PSYCHOLOGY Gillian Butler and Freda McManus
QUANTUM THEORY John Polkinghorne
ROMAN BRITAIN Peter Salway
ROUSSEAU Robert Wokler
RUSSELL A. C. Grayling
RUSSIAN LITERATURE Catriona Kelly
THE RUSSIAN REVOLUTION S. A. Smith
SCHIZOPHRENIA Chris Frith and Eve Johnstone
SCHOPENHAUER Christopher Janaway
SHAKESPEARE Germaine Greer
SOCIAL AND CULTURAL ANTHROPOLOGY John Monaghan and Peter Just
SOCIOLOGY Steve Bruce
SOCRATES C. C. W. Taylor
SPINOZA Roger Scruton
STUART BRITAIN John Morrill
TERRORISM Charles Townshend
THEOLOGY David F. Ford

Available soon:

THE TUDORS John Guy
TWENTIETH-CENTURY BRITAIN Kenneth O. Morgan
WITTGENSTEIN A. C. Grayling
WORLD MUSIC Philip Bohlman
AFRICAN HISTORY John Parker and Richard Rathbone
ANCIENT EGYPT Ian Shaw
THE BRAIN Michael O'Shea
BUDDHIST ETHICS Damien Keown
CHAOS Leonard Smith
CHRISTIANITY Linda Woodhead
CITIZENSHIP Richard Bellamy
CLASSICAL ARCHITECTURE Robert Tavernor
CLONING Arlene Judith Klotzko
CONTEMPORARY ART Julian Stallabrass
THE CRUSADES Christopher Tyerman
DERRIDA Simon Glendinning
DESIGN John Heskett
DINOSAURS David Norman
DREAMING J. Allan Hobson
ECONOMICS Partha Dasgupta
THE END OF THE WORLD Bill McGuire
EXISTENTIALISM Thomas Flynn
THE FIRST WORLD WAR Michael Howard
FREE WILL Thomas Pink
FUNDAMENTALISM Malise Ruthven
HABERMAS Gordon Finlayson
HIEROGLYPHS Penelope Wilson
HIROSHIMA B. R. Tomlinson
HUMAN EVOLUTION Bernard Wood
INTERNATIONAL RELATIONS Paul Wilkinson
JAZZ Brian Morton
MANDELA Tom Lodge
MEDICAL ETHICS Tony Hope
THE MIND Martin Davies
MYTH Robert Segal
NATIONALISM Steven Grosby
PERCEPTION Richard Gregory
PHILOSOPHY OF RELIGION Jack Copeland and Diane Proudfoot
PHOTOGRAPHY Steve Edwards
THE RAJ Denis Judd
THE RENAISSANCE Jerry Brotton
RENAISSANCE ART Geraldine Johnson
SARTRE Christina Howells
THE SPANISH CIVIL WAR Helen Graham
TRAGEDY Adrian Poole
THE TWENTIETH CENTURY Martin Conway

For more information visit our web site

www.oup.co.uk/vsi

Paul Bahn

ARCHAEOLOGY

A Very Short Introduction

with illustrations by Bill Tidy

OXFORD
UNIVERSITY PRESS

OXFORD
UNIVERSITY PRESS

Great Clarendon Street, Oxford OX2 6DP

Oxford University Press is a department of the University of Oxford.
It furthers the University's objective of excellence in research, scholarship,
and education by publishing worldwide in

Oxford New York

Auckland Bangkok Buenos Aires Cape Town Chennai
Dar es Salaam Delhi Hong Kong Istanbul Karachi Kolkata
Kuala Lumpur Madrid Melbourne Mexico City Mumbai Nairobi
São Paulo Shanghai Taipei Tokyo Toronto

Oxford is a registered trade mark of Oxford University Press
in the UK and in certain other countries

Published in the United States
by Oxford University Press Inc., New York

First published as an Oxford University Press paperback 1996
Reissued 2000

British Library Cataloguing in Publication Data
Data available

Library of Congress Cataloging in Publication Data
Data available

ISBN 978-0-19-285379-0

13 15 17 19 20 18 16 14

Typeset by RefineCatch Ltd., Bungay, Suffolk
Printed in Great Britain by
Ashford Colour Press Ltd, Gosport, Hants.

For Ann, Steve, James, and Philip

Preface

Exactly forty years ago, Vere Gordon Childe – one of this century's foremost prehistorians as well as one of the subject's greatest eccentrics – published a book called *A Short Introduction to Archaeology*. The present volume has no pretensions to equal its predecessor except in brevity.

Indeed, this little book is merely intended to whet the appetite by presenting some rudiments of the subject of archaeology in the hope that the reader may be stimulated to delve more deeply into its rich literature, to carry out some research or fieldwork, or, in the case of students, decide to take it up as a university course. You may not find employment at the end of such a course, or even at the end of a Ph.D.; but in these days when even the 'safe' areas like banking no longer guarantee a job for life, you might as well enjoy yourself while you can, and – as the late Glyn Daniel often emphasized – archaeology is nothing if it is not about pleasure. Inevitably you may need to shift and sieve a lot of earth, memorize some boring dates, wrap your tongue round meaningless jargon, and try to grapple with the Sumo wrestlers of theory, but at the same time you will be transported into a world of art and artefacts, temples and tools, tombs and treasures, lost cities and mysterious scripts, mummies and mammoths . . . And although such things are scorned or dismissed by purists as vulgar and unrepresentative of modern archaeology, it would be a strange youngster indeed who was not first turned on to the subject by its exciting or spectacular aspects.

If you were to ask members of the educated public, in any country in the world today, to name a living archaeologist, it is a safe bet that hardly any of them would come up with a single example other than the fictional Indiana Jones. Such is the power of Hollywood, and such is the anonymity of present-day archaeology. The great characters of the past are all gone – we shall probably not see their like again – but an army of mildly eccentric and dedicated professionals and amateurs are hard at work around the globe, trying to make sense of the past. You too could join their ranks, and this book may help you decide whether you're cut out for the job. If you want to became a professional, there are three basic routes: do a university course in archaeology, do a course in museum studies, or find employment in a regional unit or (in America) in Cultural Resource Management to gain practical experience. You may never become a great archaeologist, but if you can't do something well, just learn to enjoy doing it badly.

Oh, and don't expect to get rich.

'GREAT ARCHAEOLOGISTS OF THE PAST' DIG
SIR HERBERT FROOM
F.S.A.
1873-1968

Contents

List of Illustrations

Introduction

> There are few hobbies that tend to make one so healthy and philosophic as that of prehistoric archaeology.
>
> (*The Times*, 18 January 1924)

In *The Secret People*, one of his lesser known early novels, John Wyndham had one character say: 'He's an arch . . ., arch . . ., anyway he digs for things which aren't no manner of good to anybody.' That is certainly a radical view, and a widespread one at that, of what archaeologists do. At the other extreme one can wax lyrical, like Carsten Niebuhr, that 'He who calls what has vanished back again into being enjoys a bliss like that of creating' – and certainly some archaeologists are so proud of their 'creations' that they consider themselves to be godlike in many ways.

To the general public, archaeology tends to be synonymous with digging, as if this is what practitioners of the subject do all the time: in the British satirical magazine *Private Eye*, any archaeologist is automatically described as 'Man with beard in hole'. Cartoons usually depict archaeologists as crusty old fogies, covered in cobwebs, and obsessed with old bones and cracked pots. Of course, all of this is perfectly accurate, but it only reflects a very small part of the subject. Some archaeologists never excavate, for example, and very few of them spend most of their time at it.

So what exactly *is* archaeology? The word comes from the Greek (*arkhaiologia*, 'discourse about ancient things'), but today it has come to mean the study of the human past through the material traces of it that have survived. The term *human* past needs stressing, because archaeologists do *not* – contrary to what many of the public believe, thanks to the Flintstones, and Raquel Welch in that memorable fur bikini – study dinosaurs, or rocks *per se*. Those are the realm of palaeontologists and geologists; dinosaurs had been extinct for tens of millions of years when the first humans evolved.

Archaeology starts, really, at the point when the first recognizable 'artefacts' (tools) appear – on current evidence, that was in East Africa about 2.5 million years ago – and stretches right up to the present day. What you threw in the garbage yesterday, no matter how useless, disgusting, or potentially embarrassing, has now become part of the recent archaeological record. Although the majority of archaeologists study the remote past (centuries or thousands of years back in time), increasing numbers are turning to historical periods and even quite modern phenomena – for example the Nevada nuclear test-site, the huts of Polar explorers, and even Nazi bunkers and the Berlin Wall have attracted the attention of archaeologists lately!

In the late sixteenth century, William Camden, the first great English antiquary, described the study of antiquities as a 'back-looking curiositie' – in other words, a desire to know about the past – and many of the people who are involved in it are certainly curious in every sense. It is a subject that seems to act like a magnet to eccentrics, but its vast span ensures that it contains something to suit all types. The shy, lonely introvert finds contentment shut up in some dusty room, poring over old coins or bits of pot or stone, while the brash extrovert can spend weeks out in the field surrounded by a large team of unbelievably hearty people.

One of the joys of archaeology is that the whole world is your oyster, providing you can raise the funding to do the work. You can stick a pin in the globe, or choose any time-period to focus on: there will always be some archaeological problem to investigate, be it in dense jungles, deep caves, burning deserts, or freezing mountains. Nor do you need to be limited to the land – if such is your bent, you can become an underwater archaeologist or specialize in aerial photography. Since the subject encompasses all of our history, you have the whole gamut from fossil humans to the medieval or industrial periods from which to choose; anything and everything from studying the crudest pebble tools, barely distinguishable from natural stones, to analysing satellite photographs for data on archaeological sites.

You may choose to excavate intensively, or carry out extensive surface surveys, spend your time on the classification of different types of objects, or the most abstract kind of theorizing, telling everyone where they are going wrong and how nothing is correct. You can spend your time in a library or a laboratory. You may work in a museum or a regional archaeological unit, devote your life to teaching or to original research (a few people even manage both), or you can stay outside the 'profession' and be branded an 'amateur' or 'avocational archaeologist': 'amateurs' have made a huge contribution to archaeology over the years, and continue to do so, although the occupants of academia's ivory towers often patronize and sneer at them. In fact many 'amateurs' can be far more knowledgeable than the 'professionals' and often far more dedicated than those who see archaeology as merely a career, or a way of earning a living rather than as something which fires their passions, and consumes their weekends and every scrap of spare time. Naturally, this can be taken too far, and there is nothing worse or more tedious than those – professionals or amateurs – for whom archaeology is an all-devouring obsession. It helps to keep the subject in perspective, and remind oneself that we are basically just nosing around in dead people's left-overs and trying to guess how they lived their lives.

If you fancy a fairly active or exotic approach, but don't wish (or have the ability or funding) to excavate or survey, there are plenty of alternatives: for example, experimental archaeology, or 'ethnoarchaeology' (see p. 28), or rock art research. You can stay in your armchair, or travel the world, practising your language skills in either case. You may need to investigate the behaviour and habits of wild animals, or the rudiments of farming; you may find it useful to consult people who are experts in traditional crafts such as stonemasonry, woodworking, shipbuilding, or potting, or who are skilled in navigation or astronomy. In other words, doing archaeology is like going to a whole battery of evening classes all at once.

The range of possibilities is endless, so inevitably this short book will be very far from exhaustive. It can take a look at only a few of the main areas of concern of present-day archaeology, to whet your appetite and stimulate your own back-looking curiosity.

One of the qualities most archaeologists need to have in abundance, regardless of their speciality, is optimism – i.e. the belief that they can say something meaningful about the past based simply on its material remains. The basic problem they face is that very little evidence survives of most of the things that ever happened in the past, and of this evidence only the tiniest fraction is ever recovered by archaeologists, and probably only a minute portion of what is recovered is correctly interpreted or identified. But don't let this put you off – on the contrary, most people use this situation to their advantage: some by devoting time to drawing lines through gaps in the evidence to produce sequences of phases or types; others by simply ignoring how terrible and unrepresentative the data are, and using them regardless to produce stories about the past. As Harvard biologist Stephen Jay Gould has written, 'So much of science proceeds by telling stories – in the good sense, but stories nonetheless. Consider the traditional scenarios of human evolution – tales of the hunt, of campfires, dark caves, rituals, and toolmaking, coming of age, struggle and death. How much is based on bones and artifacts and how much on the norms of literature?'

THERE'S ONLY YOU AND ME LEFT, COLONEL!

You might think you're on safer ground with historical archaeology, but not a bit of it. Naturally we know more about some aspects of these cultures because they left written records, but all historians know that you still have to take bias and inaccuracy into account. For example, all the surviving texts and eyewitness accounts concerning Custer's crushing defeat at the Battle of the Little Bighorn – which took place as recently as 1876 – are substantially different not only in terms of what happened and how, but even in basics such as numbers on either side. As A. J. P. Taylor said, history is not a catalogue but a version of events.

One can, of course, also find pessimists among the ranks of archaeologists – those who believe that the waste products they study have no use, and that, in a sense, the same is true of themselves. Archaeology is undeniably a 'luxury' subject, which constantly needs to justify its existence (p. 93), but at the same time it is one which the majority of the general public find fascinating and entertaining, as shown by its consistently high viewing figures on television (especially if Egypt is involved), and which contributes immeasurably to world tourism (p. 95).

In more personal terms, it is a subject in which one can thoroughly enjoy one's work, and meet or be in close touch with scores of friendly and like-minded people around the globe, particularly at conferences. Conversely, the degree of territoriality, bitchiness, backstabbing, and vicious infighting for some reason goes way beyond what is normally encountered in other disciplines. If you are planning to enter this field, you need the hide of a rhinoceros. There are inevitably a few archaeologists who are pompous, hypocritical, dishonest, pretentious, self-promoting, and unprincipled, but that does not stop them doing well in the profession. Quite the contrary, in fact. (Alas, I'm unable to name some examples here, much as I would like to, but they know who they are.)

So – to sum up – archaeology is the very broadest of churches, with something to offer everyone, and which welcomes everybody – even, or especially, misfits, nerds, and the socially challenged who should find it more fulfilling than trainspotting or surfing the Internet.

Since nobody *knows* what happened in the past (including the recent historical past), there will never be an end to archaeological research. Theories will come and go, and new evidence or discoveries will alter the accepted fiction that constitutes the orthodox view of the past and which becomes established through general repetition and widespread acceptance. As Max Planck wrote, 'A scientific truth does not triumph by convincing its opponents and making them see the light, but rather because its opponents die and a new generation grows up that is familiar with it.'

Archaeology is a perpetual search, never really a finding; it is an eternal journey, with no true arrival. Everything is tentative, nothing is final.

Lest the above sound a trifle jaundiced, rest assured that archaeology remains tremendous fun, and can be so exciting that a truly extraordinary find like the Iceman or the Terracotta Army can ignite the interest of the whole world. Few other subjects can say as much.

Chapter 1
The Origins and Development of Archaeology

Archaeology – like nostalgia – is not what it used to be, so where did it come from? What is the 'archaeology of archaeology'?

Most human beings have some interest in the past: indeed, together with the fact that we know we are going to die and that we are uniquely capable of destroying our planet this may be one of humankind's distinguishing characteristics. It seems likely that humans have always been curious about the traces left by their predecessors – we can never know when this began, but there are many cases where ancient cultures seem to have collected or even venerated even more ancient objects: for example, a fifth-century Thracian princess in the Balkans had a collection of Stone Age axes in her grave. In North America; Iroquoian sites of the fifteenth and sixteenth centuries AD contain artefacts made thousands of years earlier; while in South America Inca emperors are said to have collected the spectacularly pornographic pottery of the Moche culture, already centuries old.

The earliest known 'archaeologist' was Nabonidus, king of Babylon, who, in the sixth century BC, excavated a temple floor down to a foundation stone laid thousands of years before. In D. W. Griffiths' magnificent silent epic *Intolerance* of 1916, one scene has the following caption: 'Belshazzar's father has a red letter day. He excavates a foundation brick of the temple of Naram-Sin, builded 3,200 years before. Incidentally, he remarks that Cyrus, the Persian, Babylon's mighty foe, is nearing the city.' This suggests that even the earliest pioneers of archaeology were obsessed with their subject and prone to absent-mindedness.

Not that 'archaeologists' were always like those of today. In fact, in Greece during the first centuries AD the term denoted a category of actors who recreated ancient legends on stage through dramatic mimes! The term archaeology, as understood today, was reinvented by a seventeenth-century doctor and antiquary of Lyons called Jacques Spon. He also proposed the word 'archaeography', but that one fell on stony ground.

In the Roman period, Julius Caesar's soldiers discovered many tombs of great antiquity when they were founding colonies in Italy and Greece; they rifled them for pots and bronzes, which were sold for high prices in Rome, an early example of grave-robbing and a trade in antiquities. Even the emperor Augustus was said by the historian Suetonius to have collected 'the huge skeletons of extinct sea and land monsters popularly known as "giants' bones"; and the weapons of ancient heroes'.

By medieval times, people in Europe were becoming intrigued by 'magic crocks', pots (probably cremation urns) which mysteriously emerged from the ground through erosion or the actions of burrowing animals. At the same time, humanly-worked flints and polished stone axes were constantly turning up as farmers ploughed their fields. According to popular belief, these artefacts were elf-shot or thunderbolts, and in fact they were venerated and collected by peoples as far afield as Africa and India, often being used as amulets or charms. In Europe, many found their way into the 'Cabinets of Curiosities', collections of natural and artificial objects put together by early antiquaries, and the realization slowly dawned in more enlightened minds that these 'thunderbolts' and 'magic crocks' were in fact the humanly made relics of ancient peoples. At the same time, discoveries of Greek and Roman sculpture were inspiring contemporary artists to study Classical forms, while wealthy families began to collect and display Classical antiquities.

It was in the sixteenth century that, in north-west Europe, some scholars really began to question Francis Bacon's claim that 'the most ancient times (except what is preserved of them in scriptures) are buried in silence and oblivion', and recognized that information about the ancient past could be derived from the study of field monuments; a whole series of antiquaries in Britain, Scandinavia, and elsewhere started to visit and describe monuments. The seventeenth and eighteenth centuries saw these activities grow into a more systematic interest, accompanied by increasing numbers of excavations. While most digs were intended merely to retrieve objects from the ground, a few pioneers treated the work like a careful dissection, noting the relationships of artefacts to different layers of soil, and realizing that, on the whole, objects from upper layers must be younger than those from layers below.

This new approach to interrogating and reading the ground and the landscape like a document led to a craze for barrow-digging – i.e. excavating the burial mounds of north-west Europe or North America. This was above all a leisure pursuit for gentlemen, clerics, doctors, businessmen, school teachers, and the like; even today, these professions make a noble contribution to 'amateur' archaeology.

It was really only in the early to mid-nineteenth century that archaeology took over from antiquarianism, in the sense of aspiring to be systematic and scientific about the vestiges of the past. This was the period when, through discoveries in western Europe of stone tools in association with now extinct animals, the great antiquity of humankind

The excavation of *Taylors Low*, Wetton, May 1845

was first established and eventually became generally accepted. By the end of the nineteenth century, true archaeology was already a flourishing enterprise, with many of the 'greats' hard at work – Petrie in Egypt, Koldewey at Babylon, Schliemann in the Aegean, Pitt-Rivers in Britain. For most of these pioneers (with the possible exception of the slippery and mendacious Schliemann) it was no longer a treasure-hunt but a search for information, and a means of answering specific questions.

Through the twentieth century, thanks to the efforts of a whole series of major figures such as Wheeler in Britain and India, Reisner and Woolley in the Near East, Uhle and Kidder in America, Bordes and Leroi-Gourhan in France, it has become a massive, multi-disciplinary undertaking, drawing on the expertise of innumerable fields – from geophysicists (who can detect something of what lies beneath the ground with a series of gadgets) and aerial photographers, to zoologists, botanists, chemists, geneticists, and a whole gamut of scientists who can produce dates from archaeological material or from the sediments that enclose it (p. 17).

There have been two major trends over time: first, excavation has become far slower and more painstaking. Instead of setting about the archaeological layers with pickaxes (or even explosives!) as in the past, each layer is carefully shovelled, scraped, or brushed away, and everything is sieved, so as not to lose any scrap of information the earth might hold. For instance, down the 'Pit of Bones' at Atapuerca, Spain, a chamber deep inside a cave, that holds the skeletons of scores of people from at least 200,000 years ago (in fact, this appears to be the world's oldest known funerary ritual – see p. 43), the excavators remove only about 10 inches of soil each July. This yields around 300 human bones, which are all they can handle since each has to be cleaned and hardened and conserved. The work is incredibly meticulous, and the remaining sediments are washed and sieved so carefully that even the tiny bones of the inner ear have been recovered.

The second major trend is that, ironically, we are not only acquiring vastly increased quantities of material of all kinds, but – thanks to the development of new techniques and scientific analyses – we can now learn far more from each object. Take, for instance, a single potsherd (fragments of pottery are among the most durable and hence most ubiquitous kinds of archaeological evidence): in the past, a sherd would simply have been classed as a type, based on its shape, material and decoration, if any. Now, however, one can obtain a detailed breakdown of its raw materials, enabling their source to be pinpointed; one can learn at what temperature it was fired, and with what material it was tempered; the pot itself can be dated by the technique of thermoluminescence (see p. 22), and other methods can be used to analyse the faintest traces of residues on its inner surface, and thus tell us what it used to contain!

In other words, as archaeology develops, it is doing much more with far less. It is also, alas, producing far too much in every sense. There are ever-growing numbers of archaeologists all over the world, competing for positions, and all trying to produce information or new data. Huge numbers of conferences and symposia are being held, most of which eventually have their proceedings published in book form. Consequently, the subject's literature is out of control, a vast multi-headed Hydra with new journals and series of monographs springing up every year, which few can afford and which even libraries are hard-pressed to buy in these days of shrinking budgets. Nobody can hope to keep up with all the literature on a single period or region or speciality, let alone on the archaeology of a continent, and still less of the whole world.

Things were very different before the War. If you take a look at the original doctoral dissertations of such great names as Grahame Clark or Glyn Daniel in Cambridge's University Library, you will find that they are very slim volumes indeed, barely equivalent to a single thesis chapter in the 1990s. Of course, there was a lot less archaeology to learn and read in their student days, and they did not have the luxury of the great gods Xerox and Apple, and had to rely on taking notes and copying maps by hand.

At the same time, museums are full to overflowing, with conservation becoming an increasing problem (see p. 99). In Egypt, for example, archaeologists have even taken to reburying objects in the knowledge that they will survive better and longer, for future generations to look at, if entrusted to mother earth rather than to museum cellars or warehouses. Just as there is a huge backlog of unpublished excavations, so there is an 'artefact mountain', a vast collection of uncatalogued and/or unstudied objects in the world's museums. Things are so bad that Naples Museum had to shut its doors recently because thousands of coins and other objects were disappearing from its storerooms where less than half the stock is catalogued. There is clearly much to do, if archaeology is to put its supremely untidy and overstuffed house in order

Archaeology as a Separate Subject

Since the renewed optimism of the 1960s (p. 68) archaeologists have had much greater confidence in their subject's ability to make a unique contribution to the study of human behaviour, and this was especially important in North America, in view of archaeology's relationship there with sister disciplines.

Anthropology simply means the study of humanity; in Britain it is divided into social (or cultural) anthropology, which analyses human culture and society; and physical (or biological) anthropology, which studies human physical characteristics and how they have evolved. In America, however, archaeology is also considered to be very much an integral part of anthropology: most academic archaeologists are to be found in 'Departments of Anthropology', where the subject is treated as a sub-discipline, rather than as a field in its own right as it is in the Old World.

Archaeology has been called 'the past tense of Cultural Anthropology', and, since it deals with the human past, it is undeniably an aspect of anthropology. However, it is equally a part of history – in fact, history could reasonably be described as the tip of archaeology's iceberg, since for more than 99 per cent of the human past archaeology is the only real source of information. History (apart from oral history) only begins with the introduction of written records around 3000 BC in western Asia and much later in most parts of the world. And even for the historical periods, information derived from archaeological data is still an invaluable complement to what is known from texts – and in any case it is often the archaeologist who unearths the documents and inscriptions in the first place.

One fundamental difference, of course, between anthropology and archaeology is that anthropologists, by and large, have an easy time of it, able to observe behaviour and interview informants because anthropology happens in the present. (Some pedants in 'Post-processual archaeology' (see p. 71), of course, have pointed out that there is no such thing as the present, since as soon as you become conscious of a moment it is already in the past. This kind of facile observation, however, merely invites a loud raspberry.) Archaeology's 'informants' are dead, and its evidence far more mute – answers need to be coaxed out. It is almost the difference between chatting to a bright, sharp youth on the one hand, and a corpse on the other!

Another corollary of this difference is that whereas anthropologists can *see* how their subjects behave and ask for explanations, archaeologists have to reconstruct behaviour. In order to do this, they need to make the massive assumption that human behaviour has remained unchanged since at least the appearance of 'anatomically modern humans' perhaps 100,000 years ago, and is therefore predictable. Exactly the same kind of assumptions have to be made about the animals and plants they exploited: i.e. that their behaviour, tastes, tolerances of climate and environment or soil and humidity have always been the same and can therefore be reliably predicted when reconstructing the past. These are enormous assumptions to make, especially as we can never be sure they are justified, but they are crucial because without them archaeology simply could not function. If we cannot guess with some accuracy how humans in the past would have reacted in a given set of circumstances, we might as well give up the challenge and become anthropologists – it's far less of a headache.

Chapter 2
Making a Date

Studying the past is of little point if you don't know how old things are, or at least which ones are older than others. No amount of enthusiasm for the subject can substitute for a solid chronology – it's no use having the inclination if you haven't got the time. So how do archaeologists get dates?

Until fairly recently, there were only two ways of establishing a chronology – relative dating (which does not mean going out with your cousin) and historical dating. Relative dating simply involves placing things – objects, deposits, events, cultures – into a sequence, some being younger, others older. Historical dates came from periods from which there is written evidence, such as medieval or Roman times. For prehistory, only relative dating was available, so – although one could tell that the Bronze Age preceded the Iron Age, and the Stone Age was earlier than the Bronze, one had no idea by how much.

The basic reasoning behind relative dating came from stratigraphy, the study of how layers or deposits occur one above the other. By and large, the underlying level was laid down first and therefore predates the overlying layer. And the same applies to objects found within these layers unless there has been some disturbance, for example by burrowing animals or grave-digging, rubbish pits or erosion and re-deposition.

There are ways of finding out if the bones in a layer are of the same age by chemical dating. Over time, a buried bone's nitrogen content declines, and it gradually absorbs fluorine and uranium. So measuring these elements will indicate if a group of bones are contemporaneous or of different periods. This was the method used in the early 1950s to expose the Piltdown fraud – a supposed 'missing link' between apes and humans 'found' in Sussex in 1912, but proved to be a complete hoax. Chemical dating showed that the skull was recent, and the jaw was from a modern orang-utan. They had been stained, and the teeth filed, to make them look old and convincing. Debate still rages endlessly and quite tediously about who was or were responsible for this prank.

The other major archaeological kind of relative dating is 'typology', the grouping of objects into types which share the same attributes of material, shape, and/or decoration. This whole system rests on two basic ideas: first, that objects from a given time and place share a recognizable style (like goes with like), and that changes in style are fairly gradual. In actual fact, different styles can coexist, individual styles can last a long time, and changes can occur quite fast, but the good thing about short introductory books is that there's no room to go into such complications!

In any case, generations of archaeologists – most notably those from Germanic countries – devoted their lives to establishing detailed sequences of pot, tool, and weapon forms, and then trying to connect the sequences from different regions. Whole collections of different but contemporaneous objects can be lumped together in an 'assemblage' and assemblages too can be arranged in sequences and compared from area to area.

Other relative chronologies were based on the succession of climatic phases for the Ice Age (glacials, or phases of glacial advance; interglacials, or warmer interludes; and minor fluctuations known as stadials and interstadials), but we now know – thanks to detailed climatic information from ice cores in the Arctic and Antarctic – that Ice

Age climate was far more complex and fluctuating than had been realized. Pollen from deposits also produces sequences of climatic and vegetational change, but these tend to be fairly localized. And faunal dating – based on the presence of the bones of different animal species – was also an important method, particularly for Pleistocene archaeology (the study of the last Ice Age), as 'cold' and 'warm' species came and went with climatic and environmental changes.

Producing sequences is all very well, but calendar dates – 'absolute dates' – are what archaeologists have always craved. Until this century, the only dates available were those obtained from archaeological connections with the chronologies and calendars established by ancient peoples, and these are still of huge importance today. Many of these calendars – such as those of the Romans, Egyptians, Chinese, etc. – were based on the years of rule of their consuls, emperors, kings, or 'dynasties'. The Egyptian dynasties, for example, can be dated by working back from the conquest of Egypt by Alexander the Great which, from Greek historians, we know took place in 332 BC. Further detail and clarification came from Egyptian records of astronomical events whose dates we also know from independent scientific sources.

The Maya of Mesoamerica had an extremely elaborate calendar which was based not on rulers or dynasties but on cycles of 260 and 365 days, and a long count starting in August 3113 BC (by our own system).

This all gives archaeologists the chance to date certain objects such as inscriptions referring to events or rulers, and of course coins of the Roman and medieval periods that carry the name of the current ruler. One always has to bear in mind, of course, that dating the object does not necessarily date the layer in which it is found – a coin can be passed around or hoarded for decades or centuries – but it does at least give you a maximum age for the layer: it can't be older than the date on the coin (unless the coin is intrusive) but could be much younger.

Apart from these historical and calendrical ages, archaeology was helpless until science presented it with a whole series of ways to obtain 'absolute dates' from different materials. A (fairly) firm chronology has been science's greatest gift to archaeology (as is well known, there's no present like the time . . .).

Before the War, only two very localized techniques were available – the 'varves' of Scandinavia and the tree-rings of the American South-West. Varves is a Swedish term for the clay deposits laid down annually by melting ice sheets. They vary in thickness from year to year, with a warm year causing increased melting and hence a thick layer. By measuring the successive thicknesses of a series and comparing it with the pattern in other areas, long sequences can be linked together that stretch back thousands of years. Exactly the same is true of the annual growth-rings in trees – a sequence of thicker and thinner rings, caused by local climatic fluctuations, can be built up by overlapping samples from trees of different ages. We now have unbroken sequences stretching back to 8000 BC in Germany, for example, with which ancient timbers can be compared and their age pinpointed.

Naturally, the technique is most applicable in areas like the American South-West where the aridity has preserved lots of ancient wood, or in north-west Europe where waterlogged timbers are abundant in boggy regions. Results of amazing precision are now emerging – in Britain, for example, analysis of timber from a plank walkway known as the 'Sweet Track' in Somerset, constructed across a swamp, suggests that it was built during the winter of 3807/3806 BC.

The tree-ring method is also of immense value in acting as a means of checking dates obtained from Radiocarbon, the method which revolutionized archaeology but which also proved 'too good to be true', in a sense. Samples consist of organic materials from archaeological sites, such as charcoal, wood, seeds, and human or animal bone, because the

The Sweet Track, Somerset Levels

method measures the tiny amount of the radioactive isotope Carbon 14 (C14) left in organic substances – having absorbed it throughout their lives, they steadily lose it after they die. In a recent development known as Accelerator Mass Spectrometry (AMS), only very tiny samples are required, and the atoms of C14 are counted directly. The limit of reliable dates is still about 50,000 years.

The basic assumption behind the Radiocarbon method – that the concentration of C14 in the atmosphere has always been constant – eventually proved to be false, and we now know that it has varied through time, largely due to changes in the Earth's magnetic field. If the method had been tested on tree-rings of known age, things might have gone more smoothly from the start, and these awkward problems ironed out. Plotting Radiocarbon ages against tree-ring ages has led to the production of 'calibration curves', graphs that show the changing degrees of error in C14 dates over time, back to *c.*7000 BC.

Despite all these uncertainties, and the ever-present dangers of contamination of samples, Radiocarbon dating has become archaeology's most useful and ubiquitous tool, establishing chronologies for areas which previously lacked timescales of any kind. It can be used anywhere, regardless of climate, as long as there is organic material available.

But what happens if *no* organic material survives in a site? Until recently, this would have destroyed any hope of obtaining a date, but not any more, thanks to the wonders of modern science. For early sites, such as those in East Africa with fossil humans, the Potassium/Argon method can date rocks in volcanic areas. Elsewhere, Uranium series dating can be applied to rocks rich in calcium carbonate, such as stalagmite in caves. Thermoluminescence (TL) dating can be used on pottery, the most abundant inorganic material on archaeological sites of the last 10,000 years, and other inorganic materials such as burnt flint. Optically-stimulated luminescence (OSL) can even be used on certain sediments containing archaeological material – such as deposits in northern Australian rock shelters dated to 53,000 to 60,000 years ago, crucial evidence for the early arrival in this continent of humans. Electron Spin Resonance (ESR) can be used on human and animal teeth for periods far outside the range of C14, for example from Israeli sites up to 100,000 years old.

There are many other lesser dating methods which are far too complex and boring to explore here. In any case, archaeologists do not really need to know much about them – since most of them have difficulty understanding the scientific principles behind the pedal-bin, they have a touching and often misplaced faith in the ability of the boffins, the 'hard scientists', to take the samples of material provided and produce a suitable set of dates. One's confidence in the laboratories is not helped by the fact that, when submitting a sample for radiocarbon dating, one is usually asked to say, in advance, what kind of figure is expected! Nevertheless, as long as archaeologists know the rudiments about which methods exist, and the materials and age-range to which they are applicable, they can simply concentrate on more important issues like seeking sealed and undisturbed contexts, taking samples with extreme care, avoiding contamination, and raising the often considerable funds needed to pay the laboratories for the analyses. As any teenager knows too well, dates do not come cheap.

Chapter 3
Technology

> Give us the tools and we will finish the job.
>
> (Winston Churchill)

Archaeology has always relied enormously on the tools left behind by our forebears – everything from a chip of stone to a battleship; and for a long time, human progress was seen largely in terms of technology. In fact, scholarship chose to divide the human past into a succession of 'ages' – Stone, Bronze, and Iron, with numerous subsequent subdivisions – that was based on technological development. Although equal or greater emphasis is now placed on other aspects of the past, it is nevertheless true that tools have always been the mainstay of human existence, and all of our sophisticated computer-age gadgetry originated in the simple artefacts of our forebears. The bulk of the archaeological record is made up of humanly made artefacts.

The 'Palaeolithic', or 'Old Stone Age', encompasses over 99 per cent of the archaeological record, from the first recognizable tool about 2.5 million years ago up to about 10,000 years before the present; and stone tools are what predominate in its refuse. Unfortunately, although generations of scholars have devoted their lives to detailed analysis and classification of these rocks, we have no idea how important or unimportant they were to their makers. Stone tools are virtually indestructible, whereas organic materials – bone, antler, wood, leather,

sinews, cordage, basketry, featherwork, etc. – decay under most normal conditions. So we have lost forever most of the palaeolithic toolkit. The very name we have given to the period – 'Stone Age' – may be misleading, and it might have been more realistic to call it the 'Palaeoxylic' or 'Old Wood Age'. Certainly, analysis of the wear on many stone tools (see below) suggests that they were used simply for the procurement or working of organic materials. Which are what early technology was *really* based on.

Of course, as always in archaeology, we have to make the best of a bad job, and instead of cursing the incompleteness of what *has* come down to us ('a bad workman blames his tools') we need to work with what we have. Actually, traces of the rest do survive occasionally from the Old Stone Age – a few wooden planks and spears; a bit of rope in Lascaux cave, France; and the impression of a basket or textile on fired clay at Pavlov, a Czech site of about 26,000 years ago. For the Upper Palaeolithic (c.40,000 to 10,000 years ago) bone and antler tools also survive in considerable numbers.

In the past, stone tools were described and classified according to their shapes, their techniques of manufacture, or their assumed function. Nowadays, we know far more about some of these aspects. Studies of 'microwear' (i.e. minute traces left on the tools by their functions) owe much to pioneer work in the 1950s by Sergei Semenov of the Soviet Union, who had to rely on an ordinary microscope to peer at the various polishes and striations on stone tools. But these investigations have entered a new phase with the Scanning Electron Microscope, which allows a far closer and more detailed peek at microwear.

However, none of this is of much use if you don't know which activities produce these traces, and this is where experiments come in handy. Different kinds of stone tools have been copied, and used for specific tasks, so that the resulting traces and wear-patterns can be assessed and compared with those on archaeological specimens. In addition, the replication of stone tools – a skill which goes back to German antiquarian A. A. Rhode in 1720 – teaches a great deal about the original manufacturing techniques. Today the jargon term that is *de rigueur* (since the French long ago became pre-eminent in the field of Old Stone Age tools), is the 'chaîne opératoire', or production sequence, from raw material to finished implement. An even simpler way to gain insights into manufacture, without going to the bother of making copies, is to fit the actual stone tools back together again ('refitting' or 'conjoining') – it may be tedious and time-consuming work, like a 3-D jigsaw puzzle, but it can produce spectacular results that can enable you to follow every stage of the production process.

In some cases, one can follow the original production process by simple observation of the archaeological remains: for example, at the statue quarry on Easter Island there are hundreds of unfinished or abandoned statues which display every stage of their manufacture; at the South African site of Kasteelberg, of c. AD 950, there is a fabrication area where every step in the process of making certain bone tools can be seen; and surviving specimens of early weaving, for example from South America, can be 'read' by specialists who are able to understand exactly how they were made. Similarly, simple examination of a pottery vessel should reveal whether it was hand-coiled or thrown on a wheel. The by-products of metalworking – ingots, slag, moulds, crucibles, failed castings, scrap metal, and so forth – likewise provide clues to metallurgical methods: one bronze foundry of 500 BC in China has yielded more than 30,000 items of this kind.

Many of the experimental procedures used in the study of stone tools are also carried out when investigating the technology of other materials and of later periods – such as woodwork, fibres and textiles, pottery, glass, and different kinds of metalworking. For example, Italian researcher Francesco d'Errico has carried out experiments to establish microscopic criteria for recognizing the traces left on bone, antler, and ivory objects by long-term handling, transportation and suspension as pendants. Countless replicative experiments involving pottery and metallurgy have been carried out, and without them our knowledge of such technology would be rudimentary at best.

In fact this type of 'experimental archaeology' has now become a major branch of the subject, with whole 'villages' set up in various countries, especially in north-west Europe, to explore different techniques – housebuilding, farming, butchering, storage, and the making of pottery, stone tools or metalwork.

Naturally, even if carried on for decades, these experiments are still very ephemeral when compared to the accumulated knacks and wisdom that were passed down for centuries and millennia during the remote past; and no observation made in the present can really prove anything for certain about the past. But the limited insights which they provide are none the less interesting and useful, and besides many of these experiments can be good fun. You can release all kinds of demons lurking inside you when you are allowed to burn down a house, or attack a colleague with a bronze sword, bash hell out of a piece of stone, or smear cowdung over a wall or kiln, and call it 'Science'.

A related but less active approach to this kind of work has been dubbed 'ethnoarchaeology'. For a long time, archaeologists were frustrated at the lack of helpful information being obtained from living 'primitive' peoples by anthropologists. These fieldworkers were so obsessed with kinship systems, witchcraft, and the like, that they never bothered much with the kind of stuff that was of great interest to the archaeologists – i.e. how these people produced what would become their archaeological record. The making of pottery has proved particularly popular in ethnoarchaeological studies, but archaeologists want to know about all kinds of things: how the objects are made, when, why, and by whom; how much time and effort are invested in them; why they are decorated in certain ways; how often and in what circumstances they get broken, and how and where they are discarded – the humdrum everyday activities which tend to go unnoticed unless you're specifically interested in them, even in our own society. And archaeology is supremely interested in the trivial – the distribution of garbage, the pattern on a pot, the shape of a roof-tile.

This devotion to apparently unimportant details helps foster the impression among those outside the subject that archaeology is a parasite and a useless luxury. In a world ruled by market forces, archaeology needs to justify its existence; it needs to sing for its supper. In some areas, it finds its justification in the massive importance of tourism (see p. 96). But elsewhere, there can be great merit in a variety of practical applications: for example, 'seismic archaeology' is considered of importance in China, where ancient inscriptions and documents record past earthquakes, and in the Near East where historical, biblical, and archaeological evidence of ancient earthquakes extends back 10,000 years. Human remains may yield useful information on the history of some diseases and pathologies.

However, the most notable practical contributions lie in the realm of agricultural technology. For in a few cases, archaeologists can become almost godlike by irrigating barren deserts, or hugely increasing crop yields. They do this, however, not through their own ingenuity but by resurrecting the forgotten wisdom of our forebears. For example, the Nabataeans, who occupied Israel's forbidding Negev Desert 2,000 years ago, lived in cities and grew grapes, wheat, and olives. Aerial photographs and archaeology have combined to reveal that they did it by a cunning system of channelling rainwater from the region's rare cloudbursts into irrigation ditches and water-cisterns. Scientists have therefore been able to use the same methods to reconstruct ancient farms in the area which now produce high crop yields even in years of drought.

Even more impressive have been the events in the Altiplano of Peru and Bolivia. Aerial photography and excavation have revealed that around 1000 BC the region around Lake Titicaca had at least 200,000 acres devoted to an agricultural system based on 'raised fields', elevated planting surfaces made of soil dug from canals between them. This system was supremely well adapted to the 4,000 m. altitude, the local conditions, and the traditional root crops. However, it was abandoned after the Inca conquest 500 years ago; and modern agricultural methods involving heavy machinery, chemical fertilizers, irrigation, and imported crops have proved singularly unsuccessful in this climate. Archaeologists have cleared and refurbished some of the ancient raised fields, using only traditional tools, and planted them with potatoes and other traditional root crops. The fields have been unaffected by severe drought, frosts, and massive flooding, and crop yields are about seven times as high as in dry-farmed fields. Scores of communities, thousands of people, have now taken to the farming methods of their ancestors, thanks to the efforts of archaeologists.

Conversely, archaeology can also point to ecological disasters in the past, largely caused by people – such as the sudden collapse in AD 900 of the ancient Byzantine city of Petra, after centuries of drastic forest clearance; or the even more devastating deforestation on Easter Island, which almost destroyed that small island's unique Stone Age culture (this story was related, interwoven with a Romeo and Juliet theme, in the recent movie *Rapa Nui* which proved equally disastrous).

Another example comes from the Anasazi, who lived in the American South-West. Their settlements at Chaco Canyon were very advanced, and contained America's largest and highest buildings until the skyscraper. Begun in the tenth century AD, these structures used up the timber from more than 200,000 pines and firs. Plant remains cemented into crystallized urine in ancient packrat middens have provided a view of changes in the local vegetation over time, and it is clear that relentless woodcutting went on for centuries, not only for building materials but also to meet the fuel demands of a growing population. The resulting widespread environmental damage was irreversible, and was a major factor in the sites' abandonment. In other words, archaeology can deliver strong messages from the past, but alas, as the old saying has it, the only thing we learn from history is that we never learn from history.

Chapter 4
How Did People Live?

Much of archaeology is devoted to studying the 'lifestyles of the dead and buried', trying to assess what people looked like, how healthy they were, what they ate, and what they died of. The last two topics are not necessarily related, although the overweight wife of the Marquis of Dai, from second-century BC China, appears to have died of a heart attack caused by acute pain from her gallstones, an hour or so after devouring a big feed of watermelon (138 melon seeds were found in the stomach and intestines of her mummified corpse). Food seems to have been important to this lady, since her tomb contained numerous prepared dishes in containers, with labels attached and slips describing the composition of the dishes: a kind of Chinese undertakeaway!

Subsistence – the quest for food – is the most fundamental necessity of human life, and archaeology has developed many ways to investigate the clues to what people ate. The vast majority of these clues take the form of animal and plant remains that may be found in a human occupation site, and which are studied by zooarchaeologists and archaeobotanists respectively. They are indeed *sometimes* the residues of food that has been consumed – but not necessarily all of them. Plants, for example, can be used for many other purposes, from raw materials to drugs; animals yield useful substances such as bone, antler, horn, ivory, fat, sinew, hides, and furs; and birds offer bones and feathers. In addition, many organic remains, especially those of animals and birds, could have been brought into the site by other predators, or they could represent pets (though dogs and guinea pigs were eaten by some cultures in the past, and still are in some parts of the world).

The only indisputable proof that a plant or animal was actually eaten is its presence in a human stomach or coprolite (fossil turd). But since such finds are rare, the assumption has to be made that they were eaten; and one has to make this inference from the context or condition of the finds, such as charred grain in an oven, cut or burned bones, or residues in a vessel. It is unlikely but always theoretically possible that, for example, the occupants of a palaeolithic site full of reindeer bones were vegetarians who just happened to hate reindeer! Or who needed lots of bone, antler, and hides, but detested the meat.

Even if the assumption can plausibly be made that the remains are of food, there are further challenges to be met. For example, one has to try and figure out the relative importance of different foods: plants are commonly under-represented because their remains are often poorly preserved, if not totally absent. The same is true of fish bones. And whatever food remains do survive, one has to decide whether they are wild or domesticated; and whether they are truly representative of the occupants' diet, which can involve assessing the site's function, the duration of its occupation (short- or long-term), and whether it was lived in irregularly, seasonally, or permanently – a long-term settlement is far more likely to yield representative food remains than a kill-site or specialized camp.

In recent years, sophisticated new techniques have been developed which can detect and often identify food residues on tools and inside vessels. For example, in the Solomon Islands, Melanesia, starch residues have been found on stone tools dating back to 28,700 years ago, which constitute the world's oldest evidence for consumption of root vegetables (taro). Chemical analysis of residues in amphorae (the great storage jars of the Roman period) has proved that many did contain wine and olive oil, as had been assumed, but some contained wheat flour. Early evidence for wine – a subject very close to an archaeologist's heart – has emerged from analysis of a yellowish residue inside a pottery jar from the neolithic site of Hajji Firuz Tepe, Iran, dating to about 5400 to 5000 BC. It has been identified as tartaric acid, found in nature almost exclusively in grapes, and this has therefore been taken as evidence of a resinated wine, the earliest in the world, 2000 years older than previously thought. A 30-litre Sumerian jar from a site called Godin Depe, in western Iran, dating to *c.*3500 BC, also held wine, while potsherds from the same site bore traces of the production of barley beer, so clearly the ancient Iranians knew how to have a good time – and not only the Iranians: the tomb of one of Egypt's first kings at Abydos, dating to *c.*3150 BC, was found to contain three rooms stocked with 700 jars; chemical analysis of the yellow crusts remaining in them confirmed that they had held wine – a potential total of 1200 gallons!

Chemists have also discovered traces of opium in a 3,500-year old vase from Cyprus, which suggests to some scholars that a drug trade existed in the eastern Mediterranean at this time. In Britain, on the other hand, ancient pots tend to contain less stimulating substances, such as residues of cabbage.

Where animal remains are concerned, they too may only represent a small fraction of what was originally present: bones could be cleared out of the site, used for tools, boiled for stock, or eaten by dogs or pigs. Other possibly important foods such as grubs or blood leave no trace at all; and although we tend to assume that diet was usually based on herbivores and fish, some cultures may also have eaten insects – locusts have been found in a special oven in an Algerian rock-shelter dating to 6,200 years ago.

One area that is still problematic is cannibalism – the only way to *prove* it in the past is by finding a piece of human tissue in a human gut or coprolite, and so far nobody has done so. Recent reappraisals of archaeological and anthropological evidence for cannibalism have shown that all claims are open to other explanations, such as violence or complex funerary rituals; but a few scholars persist in interpreting human bones that are disarticulated, traumatized, or covered in cutmarks – for example in some Anasazi sites of c. AD 1100 in the American South-West – as evidence of cannibalism. They may be correct, but we really have no way of knowing; like so many things in archaeology it comes down to a question of faith and personal preference. We know only too well from recent cases that cannibalism can certainly arise among people desperate for survival (e.g. in the Andean plane crash, or in the Nazi concentration camps), and among sick psychopaths; but the very existence of 'custom cannibalism', where it is a habitual or ritual part of life, has come under serious question over the past few years: well-documented cases based on direct observation rather than hearsay or propaganda are extremely rare for historical periods, so it is very hard to estimate how common the practice might have been in prehistory, let alone the very remote past.

As with plants, animal residues are proving very enlightening, although controversy still rages over the topic of bloody stone tools, since claims that bloodstains can survive on artefacts thousands of years old and can be identified to species are contested. Chemical analysis of residues in vessels has revealed such substances as milk, cheese, and fat.

Both plant and animal foods are also well represented in art and in literature – such as wooden models from Egyptian tombs depicting baking and brewing; texts describing the food of the Roman army, Egyptian hieroglyphic texts about corn allowances for workers, or the world's oldest cookbook: three Babylonian clay tablets of 3,750 years ago which contain thirty-five recipes for a variety of rich meat stews. However, no matter how full the evidence from art and texts, they give a very short-term view of subsistence. Even shorter-term glimpses come from occasional finds of actual meals – for example in the Roman city of Pompeii, buried by a volcanic eruption in AD 79, meals of fish, eggs, bread, and nuts were unearthed intact on tables, as well as food in shops – but these are a tiny sample from a single day. The same is true of evidence recovered (by hardy souls with strong stomachs) from the alimentary tracts of preserved bodies or from human turds. The Danish Iron Age bog body, Tollund Man, was found to have eaten a gruel before death (Sir Mortimer Wheeler, in a pioneering piece of experimental archaeology, tried a reconstruction of this concoction, and found it a foul-tasting mush), whereas Britain's Lindow Man had eaten a griddle cake, a kind of rough bread. Analysis of coprolites from Lovelock Cave, Nevada, dating from 2,500 to 150 years ago, revealed the presence of seeds, fragments of bird-feathers, and fish-scales: one, from 1,000 years ago, contained bones from 101 small chubs, representing a total live weight of 208 g. (7.3 oz) – the fish course in a single person's meal.

Meals are all very well, but archaeology always likes a long-term view (that is its speciality, after all), which requires some assessment of diet. One way to approach this is to examine the accumulation of food remains through time – in the succession of stratified layers in a site – but there are far more direct methods of learning about diet: from tooth-wear and from bone chemistry. Because 'we are what we eat': diet radically affects teeth – yes, your mum was right – and also leaves characteristic chemical signatures in bones.

Teeth are made of two of the hardest tissues in the body, so they usually survive in good condition. Microscopic examination of their surfaces reveals abrasions and scratches which can be related to meat or vegetation in the diet. As with studies of microwear on tools (p. 26), we know from present-day specimens – in this case not experimental replicas but living people such as meat-eating Eskimos or vegetarian Melanesians – what kind of traces are left by different diets, so archaeological examples can be compared with these with some confidence. In this way, it has been found that fossil humans seem to have eaten less meat through time, and adopted a more mixed diet.

"BABYLONIAN RICH BEEF STEW...
DISSOLVE ONE TABLET IN 2 PINTS OF.."

Tooth decay can also be informative, indicating a reliance on starchy and sugary foods.

The greatest breakthrough, however, has come through the realization that chemical analysis of human bone collagen can reveal much about long-term diet. Different categories of plants have different ratios of certain isotopes of carbon, or nitrogen, and as the plants are eaten by animals these ratios become fixed in animal and human bone tissue. So analysis of the collagen can show whether marine or land plants predominated in the diet, and hence land or marine resources of other kinds. The technique is useful for detecting change through time, if human bones from different periods are available. For example, bones from the Orinoco floodplain in Venezuela have revealed a dramatic switch from a diet rich in one category of plant (including manioc) in 800 BC to one based on plants such as maize by AD 400.

The whole topic of investigating human remains is hugely popular with the general public, which adores the ghoulish and grisly: mummies are always big attractions in museums. However, introductory books on archaeology generally say little or nothing about the people themselves, concentrating instead on their tools, dwellings, art, and behaviour. This is a bizarre attitude: after all, if archaeology's aim is to recreate the lives of those who produced the archaeological record, what more direct evidence can there be than the very remains of the actors in the play we are trying to reconstruct?

Yet these remains have generally been left to the physical anthropologist to discuss, even though they were excavated by the archaeologist. But whoever does the analysis, the data obtained are of capital importance. Human remains can show the age and sex of the deceased, their appearance, their state of health, sometimes their cause of death, and in some cases even their family relationships. In the future, new developments in biochemistry and genetics will largely replace the present heavy reliance on bones.

The vast majority of surviving human remains are skeletal or cremations. But we do have numerous better preserved, more or less intact bodies that are desiccated, frozen, waterlogged, or purposely mummified, and these can be subjected to a vast battery of tests – forensic examinations, computer scans, and endoscopes thrust into every orifice.

Even in cases where bodies have disappeared, traces of them may be detected. The most famous examples are the hollows left by the people of Pompeii as they disintegrated inside their solidified casing of volcanic ash; when plaster is poured into these hollows, the resulting casts reveal physical appearance, hairstyles, clothing, posture and even facial expression at the moment of death (it is rumoured that the city's prison contains the remains of several hardened criminals). Numerous footprints, handprints, and painted hand stencils also exist in the archaeological record.

One particularly striking instance of vanished but detectable remains concerns the mystery posed by numerous intact but totally empty pots which have been found buried in the cellars of German houses dating from the sixteenth to the nineteenth century AD. Chemical tests of the sediments inside them revealed the presence of cholesterol (which pointed to human or animal tissue), and steroid hormones such as oestrone, so it is virtually certain that the pots were used to bury human placenta (afterbirth) – according to local folklore, this was done to ensure the children's healthy growth.

Where health is concerned, human remains can be a mine of information. For example, Repetitive Strain Injury is by no means a new phenomenon, and facets on various bones from ancient skeletons can be linked with stresses caused by crouching, load-carrying, or grinding grain. Most afflictions that lead to death leave no trace on bone, but where soft tissue has survived palaeopathology (the study of ancient disease) can reveal a great deal. Almost all Egyptian mummies

THAT'S HOW I'D LIKE TO GO!

contained parasites which caused amoebic dysentery and bilharzia, and mummies in the New World had whipworm and roundworm eggs. Parasites have also been found in human coprolites and medieval cesspits.

There may even be risks for the unwary archaeologist in handling human soft tissue – scabs and viruses can survive, and nobody knows how long microbes can lie dormant. Infectious micro-organisms may therefore pose real dangers, especially as our immunity to vanished or rare diseases has certainly declined. Lethal microbes are a far more plausible explanation for some of the (mercifully very rare) mysterious deaths among archaeologists than the ever-popular myth of the 'Mummy's Curse'. It would be ironic for an archaeologist to catch something nasty from the past, perhaps the ultimate in experimental archaeology!

Far safer is the investigation of trauma and damage, such as on the preserved bogbodies of north-west Europe, many of which clearly met violent deaths – either as executions, muggings, or ritual sacrifices. Tollund Man was hanged, Grauballe Man had his throat slit, but Britain's Lindow Man – wittily nicknamed Pete Marsh – takes the biscuit: he had his skull fractured twice, was garotted and had his jugular cut. Either he was extremely unpopular, or someone was determined to do a very thorough job.

The most ancient intact body to have come down to us is that of the Iceman, found in the Italian Alps in 1991. His discovery gained worldwide attention in the media, and immediately triggered some amazing stories, some of them probably apocryphal. For example, one women claimed it was her father who had disappeared in the mountains – she recognized him from from the press photographs! The Radiocarbon dates of 5,300 years ago soon put paid to that one. Once he was identified as a genuinely ancient body, some women allegedy volunteered to be impregnated with any frozen sperm that might be found in his body. More bizarrely, a gay magazine in Austria claimed that

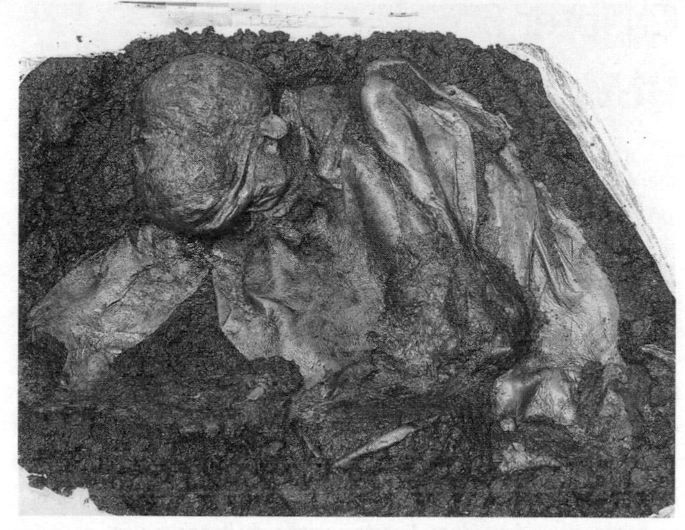

Mummified body of a man, buried in a peat bog at Lindow, Cheshire

sperm had been discovered in his anal canal, but that scientists were too embarrassed to publish this 'fact'!

The true facts about the Iceman are actually just as interesting. He was in his mid-to-late 40s. His lungs are blackened by smoke from open fires; he has hardening of the arteries and blood vessels; he has traces of chronic frostbite in one toe; and eight of his ribs were fractured, but were healed or healing when he died. Groups of tattoos on his body – mostly parallel blue lines, half an inch long – may be therapeutic, aimed at relieving the arthritis in his neck, back, and hip. But the most remarkable information came from the single surviving fingernail. Lines across it show that he underwent episodes of serious illness (when nail growth was reduced) four, three, and finally two months before his death. The fact that he was prone to periodic crippling disease probably explains how he succumbed to adverse weather and froze to death. So even in a complete body, one apparently insignificant nail can be the key to the puzzle – an apt metaphor for archaeology as a whole.

Chapter 5
How Did People Think?

Hard as it is to figure out the nuts and bolts of life – technology, subsistence, etc. – it is infinitely harder to get inside people's minds, and try to get an inkling of what they believed and how they thought. If you can't even read your spouse's thoughts (or would prefer not to!) after umpteen years of marriage, imagine what a challenge it is to reconstruct what have been called, in ghastly jargon, 'prehistoric mindways'.

This is where we turn to those brave souls who aspire to an 'archaeology of the mind' – the cognitive archaeologists, or 'coggies' as they are known, refuse to accept that ancient thoughts, beliefs, and social relations have gone for ever, and believe that they can resurrect them through logic applied to the art and material remains that are reckoned to be connected with religion and ritual or suchlike.

Many scholars are currently striving to develop explicit procedures for analysing the cognitive aspects of early societies, especially of those for which we have no written texts to help. There are numerous encouraging approaches to this seemingly impossible task. For example, one can investigate how people described and measured their world, how they planned and laid out their monuments and towns, and which materials they prized highly and presumably considered to be symbols of wealth and power. And in particular, one can tackle the material remains of religion.

It has been said with some truth that religion is, basically, humankind's attempt to communicate with the weather, and a great deal of effort in the past was devoted to this endeavour. Despite the well-known archaeological temptation to call anything 'ritual' that looks odd, it remains true, as we know from modern studies of 'primitive' people, that religious activities are often of paramount importance in life – indeed, since there is usually no clear dividing line between the sacred and the secular, much of life can seem to be ultimately devoted to religion.

The dates for some basic evidence of thought have been pushed back in recent years. For example, the deliberate burial of humans was long thought to start with the Neanderthals of Eurasia, between 100,000 and 40,000 years ago – many cases are known, one of them a famous burial in Shanidar Cave, Iraq, where the body seems to have been accompanied by flowers (judging by the pollen found with the bones). However, the finds down the Pit of Bones at Atapuerca (see p. 12) are strong indication that more than 200,000 years ago some kind of funerary ritual was being carried out, since scores of bodies were being deliberately brought here and deposited in the pit – this was not a living site (there are no tools or other remains of domestic refuse here), nor were the bodies dragged here by carnivorous animals (there are no tooth marks on the bones, all parts of the body are present, and there are no remains from other prey-animals). So in this case, one can be fairly sure merely from the content and context of the finds that some kind of rudimentary religious ritual was occurring.

The same applies to 'art'. Art is a notoriously difficult concept with which to grapple, and debate still rages over how to define it. Perhaps the simplest course is to adopt its centuries-old definition as 'the work of people as opposed to that of nature', thus avoiding any differentiation of the diversity of forms, content, or intention. As with religion, it is very difficult in many 'primitive' societies to separate 'art' from 'non-art'; such divisions have no meaning to the people, who see all their 'art' as functional, either directly as a usable artefact or indirectly as a way of communicating with spirits or the gods, or the weather, or whatever. It all has significance, meaning and function, and many peoples simply could not understand our concept of 'art' as being something separate, or special, or non-functional.

For many years, art was seen as something which began with modern humans in Europe, i.e. with the first portable art and cave-drawings of the last Ice Age. None of this has stood up to scrutiny. First, every continent now has 'art' of equal antiquity, with Australia having the world's oldest dated rock engravings (more than 40,000 years, if the AMS dates are correct); and, even more important, it is now clear that 'art' occurs well before modern humans. This was already known for decades, since a Neanderthal burial from south-west France was found covered by a stone slab with a series of little 'cupmarks' (small round hollows) carefully arranged on it. But this was always dismissed by the archaeological establishment as a freak, a 'one-off', which could not hold a candle to the wonders of later cave-art like Lascaux and Altamira.

Now, however, we not only have growing numbers of examples of simple Neanderthal 'art' of different kinds, but we have examples of even earlier occurrences. The most striking is a little pebble of volcanic rock, found at Berekhat Ram, an open-air site on the Golan Heights, Israel, in the 1980s. Its natural shape resembles a woman, but there are grooves around the 'neck' and down the 'arms', and the problem was whether these lines were also natural or humanly made. Microscopic analysis by American researcher Alexander Marshack has now proved them beyond all doubt to be artificial, so this pebble is unquestionably a 'figurine', an art object – yet it dates to at least 230,000 years ago, and possibly much more. So here, once again, we have clear evidence of

cognitive activity – the pebble's natural resemblance to a woman was recognized, and then deliberately enhanced.

Even if one adheres to the traditional dogma that true art began with the modern humans of the last Ice Age, it would nevertheless still be true that prehistoric art, and 'rock art' in particular, constitutes 99 per cent of art history. It is ironic that most books on the History of Art begin with a token photo of cave art (usually Lascaux or Altamira, neither of which is really representative) or of a female figurine (usually one of the really obese ones, which are equally unrepresentative), before moving on to the more familiar ground of Egypt and Greece. Yet Lascaux, at about 17,000 years ago, lies at the halfway mark in the history of art – and of course, in the light of the Berekhat Ram figurine, one could say that Lascaux begins the 'very late phase' of art history!

Prehistoric art not only has a huge timespan but also comprises a vast array of types and topics, from scratches on bone to wonderful polychrome paintings, from simple finger-markings on clay to sophisticated three-dimensional sculptures. So one can find everything and anything in it that one wishes; thus, those humbugs and their gullible readers, who in the 1970s proclaimed that there was evidence of extraterrestrials or ancient astronauts in the archaeological record, even found images in rock art that looked (to them at least) like spacemen!

It is fairly obvious from what we know of 'primitive' art today that prehistoric art must have been multipurpose – encompassing games, myths, narratives, graffiti, messages, creation myths, and religion. Not all of it is necessarily serious and earnest, displaying terror of the supernatural; much may be rather a celebration of life, a reflection of fun and frivolity. Some of it is public, on open view out-of-doors; some is intensely private, hidden away in recesses or deep caves. But despite this flagrant diversity, many people who study rock art – or even just Ice Age art – have an inherent tendency to put single, all-encompassing explanations on it. In fact this happens in every aspect of archaeology and it is perhaps an inbuilt fault in scholarship that as soon as one stumbles upon what seems like a good idea (usually borrowed from someone else, preferably in another discipline), there is an irresistible urge to apply it to everything in sight, and subjugate every aspect of a supremely diverse phenomenon to a steamroller interpretation.

The chosen interpretations tend to reflect contemporary obsessions and prejudices – at first prehistoric art was thought to be mindless graffiti or play activity, 'art for art's sake'. Then at the turn of the century, as accounts began to appear about what modern 'primitive' peoples did, some simplistic ideas were applied quite uncritically to prehistoric art – most notably that it had a magical purpose to help with hunting or fertility. In the 1950s, French structuralism led to new ideas about cave art having a definite and recurring structure, while the 'swinging 60s' saw a proposal that the animals in the caves were sexual symbols; the Space Age led to a focus on possible lunar notations and

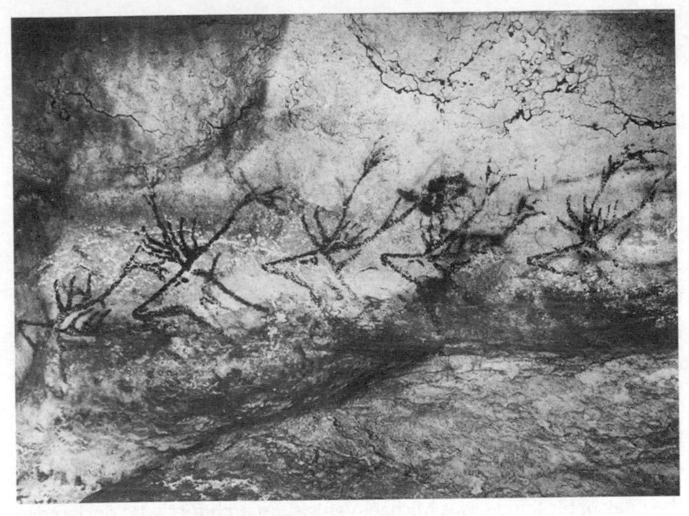

Cave painting, from Lascaux, France

other astronomical observations being perceptible in some prehistoric art and monuments. The Computer Age inevitably led to a view of rock art as being like a series of giant 'floppy disks' or CD-Roms, with information being recorded there for storage and instant recall. The currently fashionable theory that rock art consists largely of trance imagery seems to be the direct legacy of the drug culture of the late 1960s and 1970s, with its attendant interest in mysticism and shamanism, hallucinogens, altered states of consciousness, and so forth, culminating in the massive literature of the 'New Age'.

Regardless of these interpretations, all of which probably hold some truth, the fact remains that only the artist can tell you what the art represents and what its purpose was. We cannot be sure of anything. In a famous experiment, an Australian scholar asked some Aborigines to identify some animals in a rock art panel – their identifications differed markedly from those reached by western zoological reasoning: out of 22 images, the western scholars had been wrong about 15, and only superficially right about the other 7! But since we have no prehistoric informants, and shall therefore never have access to the original meaning of the art, we can only try to assess what it seems to depict and what its significance might have been.

Rock art was certainly used at times to record and transmit information. Things become far easier for the cognitive archaeologist where real scripts are concerned. But first they have to be deciphered. This is a highly specialized skill, requiring a very particular kind of analytical mind. There have been some notable pioneers, such as Champollion who first deciphered ancient Egyptian hieroglyphics (helped enormously by the discovery of the Rosetta Stone which had identical texts in Egyptian and Greek). In this century, one major figure – venerated all the more because, like some pop stars, he died young at the peak of his fame – was Michael Ventris, an architect who declared in 1952 that he had deciphered Linear B, an early script from the Aegean, as an archaic form of Greek (although the script was found on Crete, there is no truth in the tale that one tablet read 'It is a small thing but Minoan'). He was met – like most pioneers – not by congratulations but by indignant howls of denial from fellow specialists. This is par for the course in all branches of archaeology – as is the fact that when, soon afterwards, a whole library of Linear B tablets was unearthed in Greece, translations of which fully confirmed Ventris's claims, the experts were left with no alternative: they accused the excavator and Ventris of forgery!

Don't imagine that decipherment is a dying art – it is still very much alive and kicking. It is only in the last few years that the complex Maya script of Mesoamerica has begun to be properly understood after a century of cumulative research efforts, and the far rarer '*rongorongo*' script from Easter Island, which only survives on 25 pieces of wood, has been cracked – at least in terms of its structure and general content – within the past couple of years. But there is still plenty of work to be done, and the still undeciphered Linear A (of the Aegean) and the Indus script (of ancient India and Pakistan) are still major challenges for enthusiasts who wish to tease their brains.

Once texts can be read, they can obviously provide a great deal of valuable information about cognitive aspects of the past – for example, the inscriptions from Classical sites, or the first writings by colonizers, etc. However, as with history as a whole, the written word should always be seen as a complement to archaeology, never a substitute for it – this is especially true for ancient societies where writing was used for very restricted purposes, and literacy was the prerogative of an élite minority. In Classical Greece, on the other hand, literacy was widespread, and writing touched nearly all aspects of life, both private and public, so texts can provide considerable insights – for example, in identifying deities and myths in art (without Classical literature, most scenes in Greek and Roman art would mean very little to us); but, as ever, texts also incorporate biases and lack completeness.

An entire area of cognitive archaeology is taken up with archaeoastronomy – the study of ancient knowledge of celestial phenomena. As mentioned above, there may well be lunar notations from the last Ice Age (the phases of the moon would certainly have been the principal way that ancient peoples could measure the passage of time), but the subject really comes into its own in later prehistory with the phenomenon of monuments aligned on significant astronomical events such as the rising of the midwinter or midsummer sun. From the prehistoric megalithic monuments of western Europe to major buildings in the Central and South American civilizations, there are definite alignments which demonstrate a profound knowledge of, and importance attached to, the movements of the heavens.

Megalith, incidentally, is from the Greek for 'big stone' (as opposed to microlith, another important term in archaeology, used to describe very small stone tools). The simplest form of megalith is a single standing stone, like those which Obelix carries around in the Asterix comic strip –

The entry to New Grange, Ireland. Note the 'window' above the doorway through which the sun shines at dawn on the winter solstice in France and elsewhere, the correct term for such a stone is 'menhir'. In Europe, such menhirs are sometimes arranged in rows and groups or 'alignments', while in Britain, especially, they form circles or ellipses. Many of these are thought to have astronomical alignments, though it is not always possible to be certain, since there are so many things in the heavens that the chances are high that a circle of regularly or irregularly placed stones will be aligned on something significant quite by chance. Nevertheless, a number of professional astronomers in the 1960s and 1970s dazzled the largely innumerate archaeological world with complex calculations and jargon designed to prove that prehistoric people had capabilities so profound that they could construct megalithic computers – e.g. Stonehenge was a massive, accurate eclipse predictor!

Once these excesses had been debunked, the field was left open to more rational minds who have devoted a great deal of time and effort, in the face of enormous initial scepticism which was gradually transformed into a somewhat grudging acceptance, to prove that many of the European circles are indeed roughly but purposely aligned on astronomical phenomena, presumably for calendrical purposes, so farmers would know when to plant crops, and when to harvest (or should one assume that they could manage this without giant stone calendars?).

One of the main proponents of this view, a Scottish engineer, Alexander Thom, also made accurate plans of the British circles, and believed that a standard unit of measurement had been used in their layout – what he called the 'megalithic yard', or 2.72 feet. Although it is difficult to make accurate measurements in such monuments – the stones are often crude and irregularly shaped, so how do you know where to place the end of the tape-measure? – it is now generally accepted that a standard measurement was probably used. However, the most likely explanation is that, rather than resorting to sophisticated mathematics, the monument builders simply used the human pace to put their stones in place.

People too were put firmly in their place in early societies, as in today's, and this can be seen through the existence of symbols of power – ranging from giant statues of rulers (Mount Rushmore) down to rich clothing or body decoration (designer labels, diamond earrings), all of them essentially useless but considered valuable by the élite. Rare or precious materials are usually a giveaway, as are fine objects that are beautifully made but could never have been used for their apparent purpose (friable axes, sheet-bronze shields, wafer-thin stone spear-points). Burials containing such prestige goods can plausibly be interpreted as those of rich and/or powerful people, and serve to underline the hierarchy in society. The ultimate examples, of course, are the incredibly lavish tombs of rulers known in all the major civilizations – from Ur and King Tut to China's Terracotta Army and Peru's lords of Sipán – and the imposing art and architecture associated with the élite in these and other cultures. One can never be a hundred per cent certain of anything in the past, such as a simple equation of wealth with status (after all, today's incredibly wealthy rulers of Saudi Arabia are buried with nothing), but by and large it seems sensible to assume that those with rich graves were comfortably off in life too. It's important to note that the deposition of objects with the dead does not necessarily indicate any belief in an afterlife – in some cultures, it brings bad luck for someone to use a dead person's possessions, so these are buried with the deceased. The presence of food in a tomb, however, is a pretty clear indication that its occupant is expected to have a chance to take a snack after death, in the next world, and thus points to some kind of religious belief. The same is true if one finds the deceased is accompanied by servants who have been purposely slaughtered to continue their jobs for ever in the afterlife – a pretty rotten deal all round for the workforce.

Religion was often used in these societies as another means of maintaining the status quo, but its recognition in archaeological material is not always an easy task, especially where it is embedded in everyday activities. There are, however, a number of obvious clues to

SORRY, NO MORE
'AFTERLIFE' JOB
OPPORTUNITIES.
PLEASE TRY AGAIN
TOMORROW!

look for – such as a special building set apart for sacred functions, special fixtures like altars, and the paraphernalia of ritual such as gongs, bells, lamps, and so forth. Water is often involved in rites, so pools or basins may be of significance; and the sacrifice of animals or humans could be practised. Cult images and symbols can be apparent, together with depictions of people in what looks (to our eyes) like an act of adoration, while votive offerings of food or objects (often broken or hidden) may be found. Finally, important religious buildings or centres are often associated with great wealth in contents and decoration.

Any of these items on its own will not tell one very much, but if a number of them are found together, in a single archaeological context, then a cognitive archaeologist is on reasonably solid ground in interpreting the evidence as involving a cult usage. The same applies to whole collections of rich objects found in special circumstances, such as the Iron Age weapons thrown into the River Thames, or the great hoards of metalwork in Scandinavian bogs, or the huge quantities of symbolically rich objects (and people) thrown by the Maya into the cenote (well) at Chichén Itzá. It is highly unlikely – though theoretically possible – that all this material ended up in the waters through carelessness rather than through ritual deposition.

All in all, therefore, cognitive archaeology can make some valid assessments of minds which are long vanished from this earth. In other areas, however, it requires enormous optimism, and involves a triumph of mind over matter. At its best, it provides stimulating hypotheses based on historical or modern information – especially from the accounts of the Conquistadors or early missionaries and colonizers – or on careful deductions from the material remains themselves. At its worst, however, it is filled with wishful thinking, particularly where attempts to interpret prehistoric art are concerned: it produces 'just-so stories', sheer fiction thought up to explain the material remains, and through which the authors reveal themselves to be frustrated novelists.

Chapter 6
Settlement and Society

Humans have always lived in a variety of types of site, from dungheaps to palaces, and it is an important aspect of archaeology to determine what kind of settlement people occupied. It is only after discovering this basic information that one can move on to more complex questions involving the type of society they lived in.

But what exactly is a 'site' in an archaeologist's view? Basically, it is any spot on the landscape with detectable traces of human activity, or what an archaeologist believes to be human activity. So if you find some flint tools in a ploughed field, or stone axes in the Sahara, the spot automatically becomes a site. Of course, not all sites are dwelling places – for example, they may be butchering areas, or quarries for raw materials, or burials, or monuments, or rock-art sites, or sacred places where worship took place occasionally. Dwellings, even short-term ones, tend to have a diagnostic collection of traces: not only artefacts but also 'features' (i.e. non-portable elements), structures, and a range of organic and environmental remains. In particular, one would usually expect to find a fireplace – home is where the hearth is, after all.

Occupation sites range from minor scatters of artefacts denoting a brief encampment of a few hours to the enormous 'tells' or mounds in the Near East where the remains of successive towns or cities are piled up on top of each other and span thousands of years. In order to ask the right questions of the material, and to devise the means to answer them, one needs to assess the size or scale of the society, and what its internal organization was. There is little point in searching for signs of complex centralized organization in an early hunter-gatherer camp! So the first step requires examination of individual sites, and of the relationships between them, i.e. the 'settlement pattern'.

Archaeologists love to divide their data into different categories, for the sake of simplicity and to make the huge morass of information more manageable. Where chronology is concerned (Chapter 2), they tend to go for three-part systems such as Early/Middle/Late, or Lower/Middle/Upper. For societies, however, a fourfold classification tends to be used, each associated with particular kinds of site and settlement pattern. As with all archaeological terms – such as 'handaxe', 'Upper Palaeolithic', 'Neanderthal', 'Greek vase', 'Beaker Folk', or whatever – the names are descriptive, hypothetical, and completely artificial with little basis in reality; but they do serve as a convenient shorthand so that other archaeologists know to which period, or type of object, or kind of society you are referring.

The four very broad categories are: Bands, Segmentary Societies (sometimes called 'Tribes'), Chiefdoms, and States. As with archaeology's chronological divisions, these are simply arbitrary points in a continuum, and it is often very hard to assign a culture to one rather than the next, since some features appear before others. Just as nobody in the Ice Age said, 'I'm bored with the Middle Palaeolithic, isn't it about time we started the Upper?', it is likewise hard to imagine an early farmer announcing to his neighbours: 'I just want to warn you that, as from the next full moon, I intend to assume the powers of leader, and transform our cosy little segmentary society into a modern, thrusting chiefdom at the cutting edge of progress.'

1. Bands denote small-scale societies of hunters, gatherers, and fishers, usually numbering less than 100 people. They often move around with

the seasons, exploiting primarily or exclusively wild resources, so their sites tend to be seasonally occupied camps, together with smaller, more specialized activity areas such as kill or butchery sites, or work sites for making tools, often of stone.

Depending on their surroundings, they live in cave entrances or rock shelters, or construct temporary shelters of organic materials such as wood, bone, or hides. The base-camps are generally more substantial than the temporary or specialized sites. This kind of settlement is associated with the Palaeolithic period of the Old World, and the Paleo-Indian period of the New.

2. Tribes are larger than bands, numbering up to a few thousand people, and they tend to be settled farmers, though some are pastoralists with a mobile economy. Either way, their life is based primarily on domesticated resources, plants, and/or animals. They occupy settled agricultural homesteads or villages, which collectively form a settlement pattern of fairly evenly spaced sites of similar size – in other words, there is no settlement that appears to dominate. This kind of system is associated with the first farmers of both the Old and New World.

3. It is in Chiefdoms – which normally range between 5,000 and 20,000 people – that the first real signs of different social statuses become apparent, though some rich graves are known even from the last Ice Age. They are based on a ranking system, with prestige determined by how closely related one is to the chief, so there is no true class structure as yet. It is the chief who is the linch-pin of the whole system, employing craft specialists, and redistributing to his retainers and subjects the offerings of crafts and foodstuffs that are periodically paid to him (it is usually a he). Naturally, chiefs and their relatives or chums tend to have very rich grave-goods buried with them.

Chiefdoms generally have a centre of power, with temples, chiefly residences, and craft specialists. This permanent 'ceremonial centre', designed for ritual, is a central focus for the population, but it is not a city with a bureaucracy: those are features that are associated with the fourth and last stage.

4. Early States are hard to differentiate from chiefdoms, but the ruler (now a king or queen, sometimes deified) now has authority to establish laws and enforce them with an army. Society is now stratified into different classes, with the farm-workers and poor urban dwellers at the bottom, the craft specialists somewhere in the middle, and the priests and relatives of the rulers at the top. Of course, taxes are paid (in the midst of life we are in debt), so inevitably a bureaucracy is required in the central capital to administer such things: the complex redistribution of tribute and revenue to government, army, and craft specialists is one of the crucial features.

Archaeologically, one can identify an urban settlement pattern, with cities playing a prominent role – typically a large population centre with more than 5,000 inhabitants, and containing big public buildings and temples. One can often perceive a settlement hierarchy, with the capital at the heart of a network of subsidiary centres and small villages.

Archaeologists normally obtain their information about settlement pattern from a thorough study of what has already been found in an area over the years. However, in *terra incognita*, or in a region where a really thorough picture is required, the solution comes from a survey: i.e. having a territory (or a representative sample of it, if its size is excessive or if time and funds are insufficient) walked systematically by a team (usually of long-suffering students or volunteers) in order to record all archaeological traces that are visible on the surface. The concentrations of material, and their type, give some indication of the kind of sites involved, their size, time-span, and number – and, in some cases, of the hierarchy of settlements. They may be given provisional labels such as regional centre, local centre, village, hamlet, homestead, base-camp, or specialized activity area.

Some archaeologists have extended this approach to cover whole landscapes. For them, especially where mobile groups are concerned, it is no longer sufficient to locate an individual site, or even a series of sites. They also indulge in what has become known as 'off-site' or 'non-site' archaeology (unkind tongues have been known to refer to these as 'offside' and 'non-sense' archaeology), seeking the sparse scatters of artefacts – perhaps only one or two, if that, in a 10 metre square – that occur between the recognizable sites, in order to emphasize the fairly obvious fact that hunter-gatherers move around in, and exploit, entire landscapes and are liable to use and lose artefacts all over the place.

Naturally, the task of assessing settlement and society is far easier for those periods and cultures where we have written documents or even maps – these can answer many of the questions we might have about society and settlement. For example, we have thousands of early tablets or documents from the Near East, Egypt, China, the Aegean, and the Classical World detailing relationships between different sites and regions, as well as aspects of the economy – offices of state, commercial transactions – as well as of laws, royal edicts, and public announcements. From the Sumerian society of Mesopotamia, for example, we have hundreds of tablets from temples that list fields, the crops harvested in them, craftspeople, and dealings in goods such as grain and livestock. Bureaucrats have always been sticklers for keeping records.

At the other end of the scale, in sites left by mobile bands, the only record available is the archaeological one. In living areas delimited by the walls of a cave or rock shelter, the occupation deposits may be deep, built up over centuries or even many millennia, so excavation needs to focus primarily on the vertical aspect – the superimposed layers, and how their contents change through time. On the other hand, open-air sites left by hunter-gatherers tend to be far less substantial, with little depth of stratigraphy, so here the horizontal aspect is the focus of attention, tracing the distribution of fireplaces, other features, and artefact clusters.

In rare cases where one can distinguish a single, short phase of occupation at a site, it is even possible to gain some insights into precisely what people did and where, thanks to the location of artefacts, tool-making debris, animal bones, and so forth. In most sites, however, one cannot distinguish single short occupations, and instead excavators recover the accumulated evidence from repeated activities at the site over a period ranging from brief to lengthy, and with possible contributions from predators. However, this has never stopped archaeologists from using the wishful thinking for which they are renowned, and interpreting this material as if it were all from a single moment, frozen in time, like Pompeii or a shipwreck. In fact the same is true for sites from later periods; archaeologists love to conjure up stories to explain the presence and layout of what they find, in very simple terms, even though they know that the processes which created this (incredibly patchy and imperfect) record are hugely complex and usually very gradual.

In segmentary societies, survey and excavation are the basic approaches to locating sites and determining their layout and extent. Usually, in a village, some structures are excavated completely, with others being sampled to gain some idea of the range of variation. Are they all similar dwellings, or are there more specialized buildings? Within the houses, it may be possible to recognize areas for cooking, sleeping, eating, etc, and perhaps zones used by males and by females.

The analysis of grave goods or the degree of elaboration in tombs can reveal much about incipient differentiation in social status in segmentary societies, although it is not always easy to distinguish achieved status from inherited status. However, if children are buried with great wealth, it is a reasonable supposition that they inherited it rather than acquired it.

Another major source of information for these societies is their public monuments – such as the causewayed enclosures and earthen burial mounds of Neolithic Britain. For this period of the first farmers, we have lost most of the settlements because of subsequent ploughing and erosion – by and large, just a few rubbish pits or holes from timber posts have been detected – but nevertheless we can gain some insights into certain aspects of their society from an analysis of the scale and distribution of the monuments. For example, lines drawn halfway between the communal burial mounds (long barrows) divide up the landscape into roughly equal territories, suggesting that each monument was a focal point for social activities and the main burial place for the farming community that inhabited the territory around it. It has been reckoned that a group of 20 people would have needed about 50 days to construct one of these long earthen mounds, which seem to have served egalitarian societies. On the other hand, the enclosures (large circular monuments with concentric ditches) seem to be foci and periodic meeting places for a larger group of people, presumably drawn from several of these small territories – some contain stone axes that came from far-away sources. Each camp required about 100,000 hours of labour, or 250 people working for 40 days. They made their own entertainment in those days. The long winter evenings must have simply flown by . . .

Later, these camps were superseded by 'henges', a new kind of ritual enclosure (circular monuments surrounded by a ditch with external bank) which each required maybe a million hours of labour. This suggests the mobilization of large numbers of people, perhaps 300, working full time for a year or more, drawn from a bigger area. This scale of endeavour and the very existence of such major ritual centres seem to mark the transition from the simple, egalitarian societies of the first farmers to the more hierarchical chiefdoms which followed.

Stonehenge, Wiltshire

An even clearer indication of the rise of chiefdoms is the eventual filling of the landscapes around the henges (including Stonehenge, the mother of all henge monuments, which required 30 million hours to build) by circular burial mounds (round barrows) with rich grave goods reflecting the wealth of the prominent individuals inside them.

Another approach to studying the change from segmentary societies to more complex systems is through craft specialization – this also exists, of course, in band societies and can be seen in the Ice Age, since not everybody could have produced the finest stone or bone tools, or the finest carvings and rock art. In segmentary societies, craft production was primarily organized at the household level, and village sites may be found to contain pottery kilns, or slag from metalworking. However, it is in the more centralized societies of chiefdoms and states that one can see whole quarters of towns and cities devoted almost entirely to specialized crafts – stoneworking, potting, leatherworking, textiles, brewing, metal- and glassworking, and suchlike.

THE LATIN QUARTER? YOU'RE IN IT, PAL!

Where written texts are missing (as in most chiefdoms) or inadequate (as in most states), the hierarchy of sites can only be deduced by archaeological means. For example, a capital city or principal centre can be inferred from its size, and from signs of central organization such as an archive, a mint, a palace and major religious buildings, or fortifications. It can, of course, be difficult to establish the precise function of large and (presumably) public buildings, and they may well have been multi-purpose, since temples, for example, can have a social as well as a religious function. But other aspects of cities are easier to figure out – such as the areas for specialist artisans, or the differences between rich housing and slums. It is an interesting exercise to imagine the city where you live today as an abandoned ruin, with extraterrestrial archaeologists wandering around it, trying to guess what they are looking at: they too would be able to make some basic deductions fairly safely, though they might be thrown by bizarre items like photo booths, multiplex cinemas, and laundromats, all of which might look suspiciously like ritual foci.

One of the fundamental distinguishing features of centralized societies is the disparity between rich and poor, not simply in terms of basic wealth but also in access to resources, facilities, and status: in other words, in social ranking. As mentioned above, one can easily detect differences in residences and material wealth. In addition, people of high status will usually be depicted in reliefs or impressive sculptures, and of course flashy burials, as mentioned earlier, are the 'ultimate' status symbol – on the whole, the rich would not be caught dead in paupers' graves. The conspicuous display of obscene wealth is not a creation of *Forbes* or the *Tatler*, but goes back to the Pyramids and beyond. Always bear in mind that Tutankhamun was a young and minor pharaoh, so what must the treasures buried with the great ones have been like? The mind boggles . . .

Chapter 7
How and Why Did Things Change?

Perhaps the most difficult questions that face the archaeologist are those of 'why'? What brought about the changes that can be seen in ancient societies, in the archaeological record? The plurality, the vast range of present-day archaeology, the splintering of approaches to the human past, are all now reflected in the diversity of contemporary archaeological theory, a diversity which can only be seen as a strength and which is likely to lead to new insights: All avenues need to be explored, even if many of them turn out to be dead-ends. The variety is in part related to the different perceptions and preconceptions of the practitioners. Indeed, archaeology's attempts at explaining the past, and especially the changes in the past, have always varied enormously according to the predilections, politics, and social background of archaeologists, with the emphasis being placed on a single factor such as environment, climatic change, or technology, population pressure, invasions, catastrophes, and so forth.

None of these 'monocausal' explanations has proved adequate, but each probably contains some truth. In any case, different archaeologists are trying to explain different things, depending on the period, the time-scale, the type of site or the problem in which they are interested. Someone dealing with the changing distribution of Ice Age sites is likely to use a different approach from someone studying the clay tobacco pipes of a few centuries ago. So obviously, there is a whole gamut of explanations from which to choose: is one, for example, trying to examine individual events in the past, or short-term episodes, or the long-term picture, archaeology's unique speciality? Such questions could include topics like 'What destroyed this town?', 'What caused this patterning in the archaeological material?', or 'How did food production begin throughout the world?' One needs to choose one's explanation carefully to be sure it will help with the kind of problem under consideration. Fortunately, there are plenty from which to choose.

For many years; most archaeologists were quite content to answer the simpler problems of 'what', 'when', 'where', and 'how', and either ignored the harder questions or brushed them aside with simplistic explanations, focusing instead just on what they considered to be 'doing archaeology'. As Fellini once said, 'I don't know how to ask questions, and even when I do manage to ask an intelligent question, I find I am not really interested in the answer.' Yet he still came up with some pretty good movies (as well as some pretty bad ones, of course). However, in the last few decades, 'theoretical archaeology' has come into its own, particularly in North America, Britain, and Scandinavia, with everything being debated in very abstract terms. Everything had to be made more explicit: all underlying assumptions were laid bare, together with the reasoning that lay behind every stage of the interpretative process.

Other areas, such as Classical or historical archaeology, are still far more orientated towards fieldwork, analysis of texts, and the handling of real evidence. For example, some archaeologists in Germany, where very little attention has been devoted to theory, tend to consider the theoreticians as eunuchs at an orgy (especially as they are most uncertain to have any successors).

Nevertheless, archaeology has always been heavily influenced by theory, whether implicit (or even unconscious) or explicit. For example, the idea of evolution, put forward most clearly by Charles Darwin in his *Origin of Species* in 1859, provided a plausible explanation for the origin and development of humankind which had an immediate impact on the archaeologists of the time, and helped lay the foundations for the study of the typology of artefacts (p. 18). In the social sphere too, schemes of human progress were developed in the 1870s, with both Edward Tylor (in Britain) and Lewis Morgan (in America) proposing that human societies had evolved from a state of *savagery* (primitive hunting) through *barbarism* (simple farming) to *civilization* (seen as the highest form of society). There is sometimes also a fourth stage, that of decadence.

Morgan's work in particular was largely based on his knowledge of living American Indians, and his notion that people had once lived in a state of primitive communism, sharing resources equally, was in turn a strong influence on Karl Marx and Friedrich Engels in their writings on pre-capitalist societies, which later inspired the great twentieth-century Australian-born prehistorian Gordon Childe. In his later work, influenced by Marxist ideas and the (relatively recent) Marxist revolution in Russia, Childe put forward the idea that in prehistory there had been a 'neolithic revolution', that gave rise to the development of farming, and a later 'urban revolution' which led to the first towns and cities. Childe was one of the first archaeologists who really cared to tackle these thorny topics of precisely why and how things happened and changed in the past, even though he was also a supremely gifted synthesizer of data, fully at home in the more traditional pursuit of establishing chronologies and typologies. The answer to this apparent paradox may lie in his eccentricity and his wholly unconventional approach to life: only dead fish always swim with the stream.

In America, one of this century's most influential thinkers was anthropologist Julian Steward, who brought to explanations of culture change his understanding of how living cultures work. He focused not only on how cultures interact with each other, but also on how the environment could cause cultural change – what he called 'cultural ecology'. The British prehistorian Grahame Clark, from the 1930s onwards, also developed an ecological approach which departed from the traditional artefact-dominated archaeology of his contemporaries; his emphasis on how human populations adapted to their environments led him to collaborate with all kinds of specialists who could identify plant and animal remains and reconstruct past environment and subsistence in great detail. This pioneering work laid the foundations for an entire branch of modern archaeology.

By the 1960s, this kind of 'scientific' archaeology was well established, and with the rise of absolute dating methods (Chapter 2), dates could often be assigned very rapidly, and were no longer one of the principal aims of research. So it was possible to move on to, or devote far more attention to, really challenging questions rather than simply chronological or cultural ones. This is where dissatisfactions came to the surface: in a movement reminiscent of well-off teenagers rebelling against their complacent parents, some 'angry young men', especially in the American Midwest, began to denigrate the way archaeological research was being conducted, and especially – with some justification – the simplistic explanations being imposed to explain patterns in the data, such as migrations, invasions, diffusion, or vague 'influences'. Stone tools or pottery types had almost come to be seen as synonymous with peoples, moving around and interbreeding to produce new types and patterns. Naturally, migrations and invasions did indeed take place in the past (for example, the original colonization of the Pacific Islands), but they were probably not as frequent, or as straightforward to recognize in the archaeological record, as used to be thought.

The most vehement rejection came from what came to be known as the 'New Archeology' (note the American spelling), or – because of its emphasis on processual interpretations or the study of the different processes at work within a society – 'Processual Archaeology'. Leaving aside the personalities involved – who are now, ironically, themselves paunchy greybeards and considered outdated and boring by the younger generations – what were the positive aspects of this episode in archaeology's development? First, it encouraged scholars to be more optimistic (or even idealistic) about the kinds and quantity of information that could be extracted from the material traces of the past. It led to all stages of archaeological reasoning being made more explicit, so that an idea should no longer be accepted simply because X, a recognized authority or venerated master of the subject, had put it forward. Every argument must be based on a framework of logic, and on sound, testable assumptions. Above all, the emphasis was placed firmly on explanation rather than description. Instead of the simple devices of earlier archaeology (influences, migration, etc.), cultures were analysed as systems and subsystems. Great attention was devoted to relations with the environment, with subsistence and the economy, and to interactions between different social units: how different aspects of society worked and how they fitted together to help explain developments through time, and from there help establish 'regularities' of general applicability in the archaeological record.

Much of this, of course, was the natural extension of what had already been set in motion by Steward, Clark, and many other pioneers, together with the new contributions of the hard sciences and computer technology in all areas of analysis, as well as ideas imported (not always successfully or felicitously) from geography, philosophy of science, ecology, etc. In the desperate search for novelty, in fact, New Archeologists pulled in so many varied concepts from anywhere and everywhere that inevitably there were some useful nuggets among the dross and the obvious. Archaeology became like a giant sponge, soaking up and integrating bits and pieces of ideas and techniques from a whole ocean of disciplines.

Unfortunately the New Archeology's mock battles against the 'traditionalists' resembled nothing so much as the black-and-white world of party politics – rallying to the flag and criticizing everything said and done by one's opponents. Theory became a personal badge, chosen as one might choose a party or church. It meant enlisting with a group, and theories began to have groupies rather like pop stars do. The New Archeologists formed an 'in-group', so everyone else was automatically relegated to an 'out-group' – hence the vociferous condemnation of the principles and practice of the traditionalists, despised primarily for their alleged lack of theory and their unscientific approach. Yet, as Stephen Jay Gould has pointed out, silence about theory does not connote an absence of theory. The young New Archeologists failed to grasp that there are different ways of doing archaeology, all of which are legitimate and to some extent valid.

Their aggression and viciousness – not only to their opponents but also (and especially) to each other – were appalling: if you have a weak point, shout! But the two features of the New Archeologists that caused the most offence were their opinionated and patronizing arrogance, and their obscurity of language – both were unfortunate, since they masked a basic, desperate sincerity and considerably lessened the influence of the positive aspects of the approach. Jargon was all-pervading, and treated as a substitute for thought – excessive verbiage usually hides a basic lack of real information. They did not just express their ideas poorly, they simply – in many people's view – had nothing to say, and they said it, very loudly and repeatedly.

All the intemperate boasting and bullying caused hilarity when the crunch came – it is always funny to see a show-off fall flat on his face. Naturally some good came out of it all, but if you nail your colours to an ideology that goes bottom up (as they all do), you don't emerge unscathed. Over time, the anger died down, as the protagonists realized that there were no miraculous universal laws of human behaviour to be extracted from archaeological data, other than blindingly trivial and obvious ones (the most famous example was that, 'as the population of a site increases, the number of storage pits will go up'), and that most of

New Archeology had failed to live up to its numerous promises of a bright new, 'scientific' tomorrow in the reconstruction of the past. Excited and rebellious youth inevitably matured into the pragmatic realism of middle-age. For the vast majority of archaeologists – especially outside Britain and North America – it was 'business as usual'. The dogs barked, and the caravan passed.

However, the inevitable also happened, and the 'New Archeology' was soon superseded, and denigrated in its turn, by even newer approaches, and by younger Turks desperate to say something different and make their mark. Processual Archaeology was dismissed as being 'scientistic' or 'functionalist', relying on ecological explanations, and overly concerned with utilitarian aspects of life. We now have a plethora of approaches, and the subject is awash with polemical discussions between positivists, Marxists, structuralists, post-structuralists, and so on *ad nauseam*.

In particular, an approach called 'Post-processual' or Interpretive Archaeology has arisen, incorporating influences from literary studies and from various areas of history and philosophy. It rejects the generalizations that seemed to be a goal of the New Archeology, and instead lays emphasis on the uniqueness and diversity of each society and culture. In addition, it asserts that the objectivity that was another goal of the New Archeology is unattainable, and rightly stresses that there is no single or correct way to interpret the past or to undertake research. In consequence each observer is entitled to an opinion about the past, which leads inexorably to a situation of 'anything goes', where the views of the ill-informed, the charlatan, or the science-fiction writer have to be considered as valid as those of a well-informed specialist! There is also a new focus on the symbolic and cognitive aspects of the past (see Chapter 5), the ideas and beliefs of past societies, and on the actions and thoughts of long-dead individuals, with determined attempts to 'get inside their minds' – not exactly an easy task.

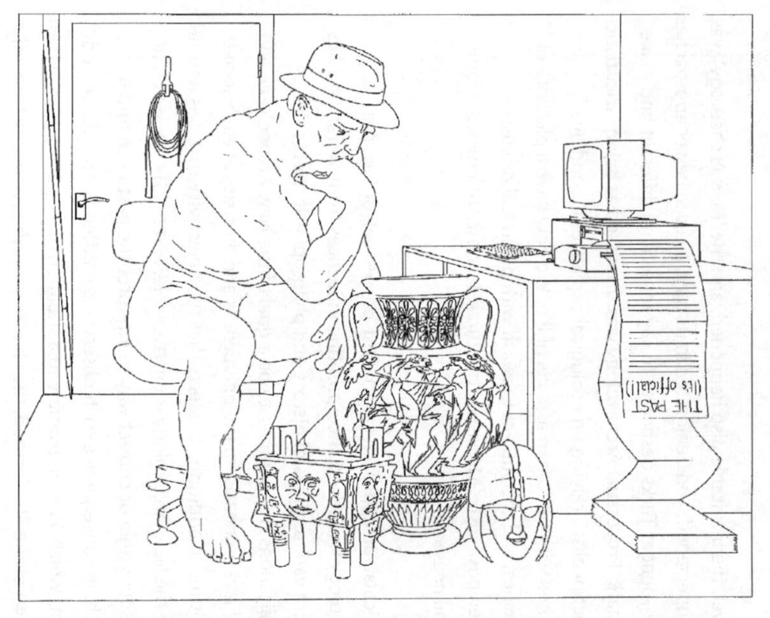

The Reality Gap (I): How some archaeologists would like others to see them (and as they would like to see themselves) . . .

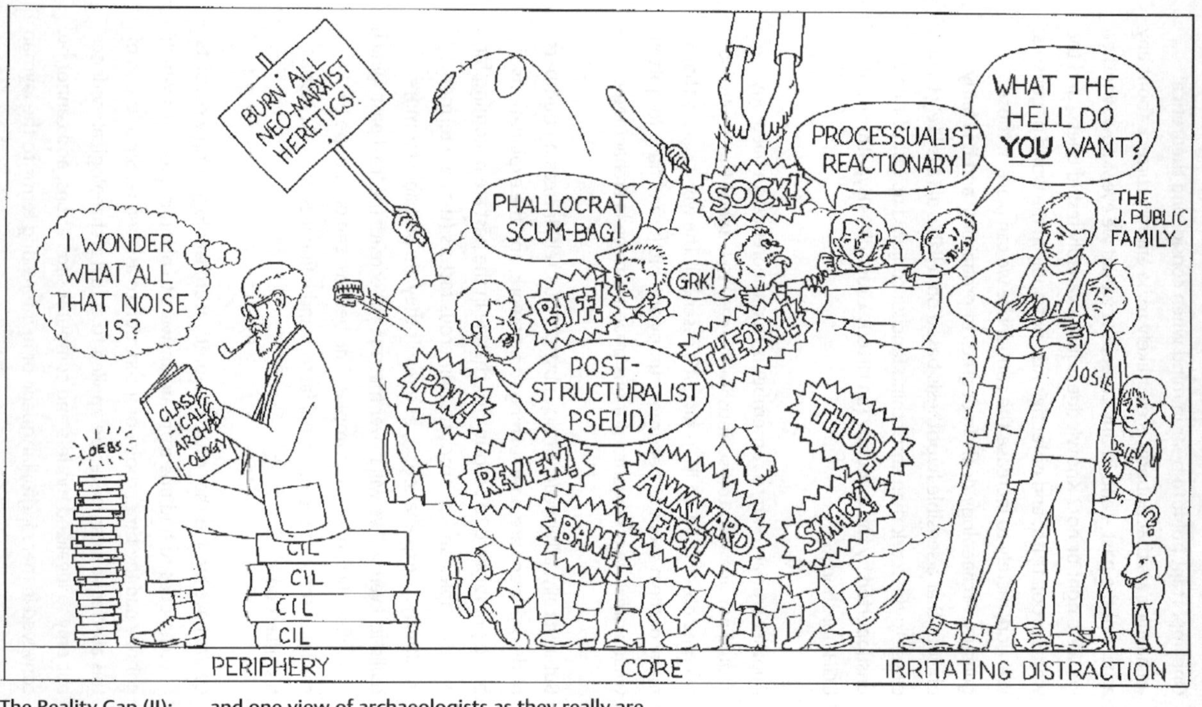

The Reality Gap (II): . . . and one view of archaeologists as they really are

One important point to bear in mind when considering theoretical archaeology is that nobody is ever likely to be entirely correct about any aspect of the past – and in any case, how would we ever know whether we were right or not? Knowledge is just a variably tested guess, and the words proof, truth, and objectivity do not apply in the world of guesses. We work merely to increase the confidence we can place in those guesses. Archaeology deals in degrees of probability, and it is fairly obvious that a sensible hypothesis based on reliable data is *likely* to be closer to the mark than something fanciful conjured up out of thin air, unsupported by the evidence (an Utterly Groundless Hypothesis, or UGH! for short).

Another crucial thing to remember is that theoretical archaeology should not be taken too seriously – it's easy to laugh at those who do become obsessed with it: in fact, it's essential. The worst part is that so many of them seem to become grumpy and bitchy and have forgotten what a great, extravagant, glorious treat it is to be in archaeology.

But ironically, after years of dry, abstract quarrels, increasing numbers of theoreticians are now turning to fieldwork, and the explanations being put forward to account for change in the past are becoming far more complex and incorporate numerous factors (they are termed 'multivariate explanations'); as a result they are probably far more realistic. Even so, we will never manage to recreate the 'real past' which was infinitely varied and complex. The best we can do is hope to elucidate some of the principal factors and influences at work, just as historians do.

Cynics have argued that much theoretical archaeology simply consists of techniques to find unsurprising answers to obvious questions which nobody had the time, tools, or inclination to ask before. Since much of this abstraction can never be applied to actual archaeological evidence but only to idealized models and computer simulations, and cannot be conveyed in meaningful language or in interesting terms to the layman

(Chapter 9) the foundations of the subject become totally neglected. The theorists of archaeology often produce beautiful and very convincing stories marred only by the fact that they do not bear the remotest resemblance to the truth or to the real world of archaeological data with which lesser mortals are trying to grapple.

Chapter 8
Minorities and Sororities

Until quite recently, archaeologists were seen – or at least saw themselves – as harmless and innocent seekers of information who could do nothing but good to the areas or countries where they worked, through bringing the past to life and recalling former glories. Since the 1970s, however, they – and anthropologists – have been vilified from all sides, which has come as something of a shock to them. They have had to face accusations of racism, Eurocentrism, neocolonialism, grave-robbing, and male chauvinism (not necessarily all at once, or in that order). The salad days are over; archaeology has come down to earth with a thud, and has had to make a long, tough, and critical examination of its practices and aims.

In the past, by and large, archaeologists – within the context of colonialism or Western dominance – felt they had the right to work or dig anywhere they pleased, to disturb the dead, and to remove human remains and sacred material to museums without the slightest permission from or consultation with local peoples, who at best were employed as guides and labourers, and at worst were totally ignored. Now, however, some indigenous groups have become not only vociferous but also powerful, especially in North America and Australia/New Zealand, and are making demands.

Some of these demands, such as the simple courtesy of consulting the local peoples and seeking their permission, advice, and help, are perfectly reasonable. As one Native American said at a conference on 'reburial' in 1989, 'You only had to knock at the front door and ask. Why did you climb through the window and steal?' Most archaeologists and anthropologists also go along with the return of recent human remains belonging to known individuals, or of particularly sacred objects (such as the war gods of the Zuni of the American South-West, which were clearly rifled, since the Zuni would *never* have consented to their removal).

The problems are arising where native demands are more wide-ranging and encompass *all* human remains (including extremely ancient specimens) or entire artefact collections. In some cases, they even reach ridiculous extremes; in the USA, for example even naturally shed strands of human hair now being recovered from archaeological sites are proclaimed by a few Native Americans to be human remains (and hence sacred), and their return has been demanded!

The Good, the Bad, and the Unethical

When I first began to study archaeology in the early 1970s, it was still a self-important and self-satisfied discipline, carried out primarily by people from the 'Top Nations' who investigated more or less whatever and wherever they chose, with only warfare and natural hazards as barriers to their free-ranging activity. I cannot recall ever encountering a word about ethics in either lectures or literature at that time. Knowledge was obtained and promulgated with an eye first to the community of archaeologists (career-advancement, peer-respect), then to the educated public, and finally – if ever – to the rest of humanity.

Ironically, archaeologists, as we have seen, not only treated artefacts as people (p. 68), with stone tool industries or pottery styles interbreeding or migrating, but also treated human remains as artefacts. Nobody sought to obtain permission from 'the bodies concerned'. Even those

The grave of a whole human skeleton with gilded spurs, at Mikuleice, southern Moravia

who espoused the 'empathetic' approach, of trying to put themselves into the minds of the long dead, saw no contradiction in their treatment of burials simply as sources of information. As Sir Mortimer Wheeler, a great empathizer, said in a television interview:

> I don't believe in disturbing rest . . . that's a mere sentimental tradition. No – if you dig up a man with bowls and things around him . . . they were dead. They had been dead a long time . . . and they were going to be dead a long time . . . they're still dead. But round them were all sorts of possessions, which were of interest to us. They helped us to put a little piece of our history into perspective, which we otherwise wouldn't have had, and so on. They enable us to reconstruct the world, and the history within which we live. And I think that's worthwhile. We do no harm to these poor chaps. When I'm dead you can dig me up ten times for all I care . . . I won't haunt you – much.

Or, as an old archaeological joke has it, 'If I should die, think only this of me, that I am an extended inhumation with grave-goods of phase B.'

By the end of the 1970s, however, the first rumblings of displeasure began to be heard from native peoples in North America and Australia, and from ultra-orthodox Jews in Israel, concerning the disturbance, study, and display of ancestral human remains. The past twenty years have seen a radical transformation of the situation, in which a once-esoteric problem has become big news and a major issue. The return of collections by museums in Australia and North America, and the holding of conferences on the problem, reveal how ethics and past misdeeds have swiftly moved to centre stage in archaeology.

In both Australia and North America, the indigenous populations were treated appallingly by the white man who generally meant them no harm, apart from wishing to take their country from them! The increased political power of the native populations over the last few decades has led to their focusing attention on the wrongdoings of the colonial period, including countless cases of sacred or burial sites being desecrated by archaeologists and anthropologists. The Aborigines and Indians were seen as laboratory specimens, and the fate of all their material – both human remains and artefacts – in numerous museums has taken on great symbolic significance. There is no single, unified indigenous tradition even within one country, since the native peoples have wide-ranging attitudes towards the dead. But since the moral case is unassailable, archaeologists have begun to right the wrongs as best they can, by returning a great deal of material for reburial or safekeeping. Codes of ethics have also been adopted in various countries, acknowledging archaeology's obligations to respect and consult with the living people whose ancestors' lives are being studied. The future lies in a mixture of acquiescence, negotiation, compromise, and the involvement of native peoples at all stages of the investigation. Working relations have improved, and there are growing numbers of indigenous people who now appreciate the contribution that archaeology can make to their history and the reconstruction of their culture.

The phase of conflict in this issue now seems to be over, and mutual respect and co-operation appear well established, except in Israel, where militant, ultra-orthodox Jews still object violently to the alleged desecration of graves. Orthodox protesters try to stop excavations by placing themselves inside burial caves, intimidating archaeologists on site, and harassing them at home by phone and mail. Excavators have been known to work at night, and send diversionary teams to 'dummy digs' to distract attention from the real site. Orthodox political parties have vowed to continue their protests over the 'defiling of our fathers' graves', and archaeologists have already had to agree to the immediate reburial of any human remains found during a dig, even though this prevents any anthropological investigation.

Corpse and Robbers

It is a fact worth repeating that by no means all past disturbance of the dead was carried out by archaeologists, nor was it limited to the remains of foreign native peoples, and some early archaeologists did have fine and noble intentions. Grave robbing, sometimes called the 'world's second oldest profession', has always been rife; in Egypt, for example, the twelfth-century BC pharaohs had to appoint a commission to inquire into the wholesale plundering of tombs in the Theban valley. Of the ordinary rock-cut tombs of Egypt, 99 per cent were looted in antiquity, and we are left with those whose contents were not worth the risk or the effort. Not a single royal tomb escaped completely, not even King Tut's.

In North America the phenomenon was under way in the time of the Pilgrims, who saw Indian grave goods as 'rotting in the ground for no good reason', and whose reaction, recorded already in 1610, was to 'liberate' the objects by robbing the graves: grave-robbing could be justified as a religious act, helping to eliminate a heathen superstition. Yet they knew that the Massachusett Indians, for example, considered it impious and inhumane to deface the monuments of the dead.

Conversely, most archaeologists do not deserve to be abused as racists and robbers. Some early excavators may indeed have been little better than looters, but the professionals of today cannot be classed with the plunderers of the past. And in any case, many burials are encountered unexpectedly and accidentally through erosion, construction and so forth, which leads to 'rescue' or 'salvage' excavations.

Human remains and burials have certainly been of major importance in the history of archaeology, but they are still only a small part of what archaeologists study. We know of more archaeological sites today than could be investigated by all living archaeologists in several lifetimes; and there is a huge backlog of unpublished excavations and material in museums and institutions. There is really no excuse for research excavation of burials today, and they have largely ceased in many parts of the world – as mentioned above, salvage excavation is now the source of most archaeological encounters with the dead. So the basic questions to be tackled are: how should salvage be carried out, and what is to be done with the remains already unearthed and curated?

The main anthropological objection to reburial of skeletal material is that no analysis is ever definitive, and that new techniques will be developed which will extract more and different types of information from the remains. This is certainly true (although it's cold comfort for the dead); but the new techniques will involve either external features (in which case a good cast should be just as instructive as the original) or internal features (such as genetic material), for which a small sample should suffice – hence, one compromise might be to keep a tooth or bone fragment from each skeleton. In any case, there will always be many thousands of skeletons available for study, which are preserved in museums around the world and which nobody wishes to rebury. In more sensitive areas, such as North America and Australia, where indigenous views on the issue vary widely, many local communities are in favour of some analysis of remains. Supplies of new specimens will not dry up, as salvage excavations will certainly continue and even increase as the pace of development and construction intensifies. So the reburial of some collections is probably less of a blow to 'Science' than it might at first appear.

Archaeology is no different from other disciplines in that it has responsibilities, and archaeologists should not ride rough-shod over other minorities. Their basic dilemma is how to reconcile a respect for the people of the past with deliberate disturbance of their remains, destruction of their tombs, and removal of their bodies and grave goods. In some ways the reburial issue is a complex problem, involving many factors, and working out the solution, timetable and details in each case can certainly be tricky. But on the whole, archaeology has been reformed – it has undergone not so much a 'loss of innocence' on this issue, but rather a realization of guilt. If bad doctors bury their mistakes, then good archaeologists should rebury theirs.

In the past, archaeologists tended to treat all objections to their research as being based on ignorance and violating some inherent and inalienable right to pursue their work wherever and however they wished. They prized their autonomy, and protected it ferociously, resenting being preached at about anything, and endeavouring to practise their profession unsupervised. Now, however, they have had to accept that other groups have legal claims on, or valid interests in, the material that archaeologists wish to examine. They are no longer the only guardians of the relics of the past, and their work carries great social implications.

Cherchez la Femme

It has been claimed, with no little justification, that archaeology has traditionally been androcentric (male orientated) not only in its basic terminology (e.g. 'early man'), but also in its emphasis on what have been thought of as male activities, as evidenced by hunting techniques and tools such as projectile points; and so it has been argued that archaeology must explicitly fight against gender-bias both in its professional practice and also in its interpretations. One hopes that we have progressed from the tone set by J. P. Droop in his book of 1915, *Archaeological Excavation*, which argued against females on excavations, since one could not in moments of stress give vent to one's true feelings in the presence of ladies! As he wrote:

> I have never seen a trained lady excavator at work . . . Of a mixed dig however I have seen something . . . before and after the excavation I thought [the ladies] charming; during it however . . . their charm was not seen . . . Marriage apart, and I can imagine a man conducting a small excavation very happily with his wife, mixed digging I think means loss of easiness in the atmosphere and consequent loss of efficiency . . . moments . . . will occur . . . when you want to say just what you think without translation, which before ladies . . . cannot be done.

Yet, even in more recent times, women have not had an easy time of it in professional archaeology. As Anna Shepard said:

> I am well aware that most people consider that a girl is not fitted for field work. As far as the 'discomforts' and 'hardships' of camp life are concerned I think the idea is a joke . . . Nevertheless because of this general belief a girl must show some special qualification to get any chance in archaeology. And the opportunity to work into field work through laboratory work has seemed the most practical.

The explicit emphasis now being placed on gender studies is therefore welcome not only for its attempt to create a much greater awareness of

THE SPHINX IS A MAN!
THE SPHINX IS A WOMAN!

the need to extend gender equality into all aspects of contemporary life, including academia, but also for the substantial contribution that it is making to our understanding of how ancient societies may have worked. However, what is called 'Gender Archaeology' is actually feminist archaeology – sisters are doing it for themselves.

The avowed aim is to focus on gender (in the sense of social and cultural, rather than biological, distinctions between the sexes) in the archaeological record. But despite assurances to the contrary it is clear that the major aim is not so much to reclaim women and men in non-sexist ways in prehistory, as to make women visible in the past. A perfectly laudable aim, and one that is highly fashionable at present, with books proliferating on Women in Prehistory, in Ancient Egypt, in the Roman period, in the Viking period, or any other era. Part of the 'feminist' approach to the past, whose goal is to shed new light on hitherto neglected aspects of the archaeological record, this phenomenon is accompanied by an ever-increasing number of conferences around the world, usually organized by or starring the same cast of characters. Although billed as concerning 'gender in archaeology', these events concentrate overwhelmingly on the female gender, and are attended by a host of female archaeologists, plus a few brave males who perhaps aspire to political correctness. The very word 'gender', therefore, is in serious danger of being hijacked, like the word 'gay' before it.

In the past the (predominantly male) authors of books or papers on archaeology routinely used the words 'man' or 'men' to mean all of humankind. One can understand that this now looks distasteful to some women (although many female archaeologists continue to use the terms, even in North America), but it was not generally done through overt sexism. I doubt if it ever occurred to the American archaeologist Robert Braidwood that his book *Prehistoric Men* (1975) could be seen as sexist. Women were, at worst, not specifically mentioned in such works, and in most cases were simply included with the men as 'people' – or, in the French literature, as 'les hommes'. (For example, a book published in 1995 by a fairly young, liberated female French archaeologist was entitled *Les Hommes au temps de Lascaux*!) Such terms did not mean males only. The new batch of books, however, is specifically omitting the male gender, which seems a deliberately sexist thing to do. The crucial difference is that between a sin of omission and one of commission.

It is true, and worth stressing, that scholars have often treated some activities as exclusively male – notably hunting, stone toolmaking, and rock art – whereas ethnography shows that women often do these things too. Male scholars either were ignorant of this fact, or chose to ignore it, and the result was a skewed version of the past. But the feminists themselves, far from shunning this practice (while justifiably complaining about it), do exactly the same by ignoring or brushing aside examples of men carrying out 'female' activities. In any case, the realization that women made stone tools will hardly produce compelling insights. Tools tell us nothing about gender: even if some future analytical technique were to detect traces of pheromones or copulins on a stone tool, or blood residues that could be identified as male or female, this would merely tell us which sex was the last to touch it; it would reveal nothing about which sex made or habitually used it.

Any detailed knowledge we have about which sex did what comes from ethnohistory and ethnography, not from archaeology. There is no alternative to reconstructing the past in this way, combining modern observations with the archaeological data. But how far can ethnography help to 'find' women in the past?

The basic problem is that ethnography can usually provide a number of possible explanations for archaeological data. It has been pointed out that even a rich female burial doesn't necessarily indicate that the occupant had any power; it could merely reflect her husband's wealth (and the opposite is equally applicable to a rich male burial, of course).

In fact it is hard to see how the respective roles of men, women, or indeed children (who are now starting to be noticed too!) could be determined from the tenuous evidence provided by archaeological excavation. The most important message of gender archaeology is that archaeology is about people – not just about men, and not just about women either.

It is utterly laudable to wish to do away with the sexism inherent in much traditional archaeology, to make people more aware of the presence and importance of women in past societies, and to produce studies focusing on women in different periods. However, in swinging away from past androcentrism, the pendulum is in danger of going to the other extreme; sexism rubs both ways. As Albert Camus once wrote, 'the slave begins by demanding justice and ends by wanting to wear a crown. He must dominate in his turn.'

The proper antidote to male chauvinism about the past is an egalitarian and neutral archaeology, not a feminist archaeology. If, as the proponents claim, they are not simply trying to make women visible in the archaeological record, is a 'feminist archaeology' needed at all? There is still a long way to go, but the *real* way forward is a balanced, non-sexist archaeology rather than a feminist kind, which is just the flip-side of the traditional coin.

Chapter 9
Presenting the Past to the Public

Archaeology's ultimate goal – if it is to have any meaning or justification – must be to convey its findings not only to students and colleagues, but above all to the public which generally footed the bill for the work and paid the salaries. Yet one still finds examples of archaeologists who are too busy to do this, or who, amazingly, do not even feel any necessity to waste their time on it. Quite recently, one of the Austrian professors who, not through any expertise but simply by being in the right place at the right time, by chance became responsible for studying the prehistoric Alpine 'Iceman' found in 1991 (one of the few archaeological finds that really interests the man in the street!) wrote that 'informing the public about his results is not really his job' – an astounding and outrageous statement for any publicly funded academic to make.

Of course, the presentation of the past to the world at large is a big responsibility, especially as it cannot be done objectively. We used to think that it could, that it was simply a matter of laying out our finds with some explanatory texts in glass cases or in books for the public's delectation. However, in recent years, as archaeologists have indulged in intense self-examination thanks to the interest in theory (Chapter 7) and thanks to being attacked from all sides (Chapter 8), they have come to realize that, through their choice of artefacts, themes, and approaches, they are constantly projecting messages that reflect their own prejudices and beliefs, or those of their society, religion, politics, or of a general world view – all under the influence of the archaeologists' own backgrounds, upbringing, and education, their social status, their interests, teachers, and friends, their political and religious beliefs, and their alliances and enmities: all these things colour their version of the past, while the actual evidence often takes a back seat.

To take just one example of how an individual's beliefs can have major ramifications, consider the story of Gabriel de Mortillet, one of the greatest French prehistorians. Born in 1821 to an old established family of Catholic monarchists, he was placed at the age of 9 in a Jesuit college. This experience greatly affected the development of his faculties, increased his already great nervous tension, and aroused in him a lifelong hatred of clerics and religion: the cane and whip were still in vigorous and enthusiastic use! As a young adult, his socialist, republican activities led to his being pursued by clericalists and monarchists alike, and he had to take refuge outside France. Eventually he became a prehistorian, and, back in Paris in 1864, founded the *Matériaux* (the world's first journal devoted to the subject) – at a time when research into the antiquity of humanity was still frowned upon by the Church. He was fighting for a fine and just cause. Unfortunately, he also had an appalling personality; he was aggressive and ill-tempered, and often academically dishonest, with a taste for personal vendettas, petty revenge, and violent language, and was unable to tolerate the slightest contradiction. The various journals he created later, usually aimed at destroying rival publications, were shockingly partial, publishing and overpraising the work of his pupils and allies, and ignoring or denigrating other scholars. He was indifferent to all new theories because he believed that if they did not fit his own they were wrong. Eventually, his argumentative and tyrannical nature caused a vacuum around him, since he had closed his mind and thought himself infallible.

Although many of de Mortillet's personality defects are still to be found among leading archaeologists today, it is his antagonism to the Church which is most relevant here because of its profound and lasting effects.

Altamira cave painting: Standing Bison

Although a champion of evolution, he never considered that religion might have evolved like stone tools, or that it might be a natural product of the human mind – instead he obstinately stuck to the belief that it was a deceit, a swindle invented and propagated by priests in the neolithic period. Since burial was generally associated with the existence of religious ideas, he decreed, against all the evidence, that there were no inhumations before the Neolithic, and every single palaeolithic burial encountered was systematically rejected as being intrusive from later periods. Until his death his best-selling books on prehistory maintained the bizarre notion that for hundreds of thousands of years before the Neolithic people were entirely bereft of the slightest trace of religion.

Even more serious was his reaction to Ice Age cave art: perhaps it was too reminiscent of frescoes in temples or churches! He immediately cast doubt on its very existence, and, when the first claims for the painted ceiling in the Spanish cave of Altamira were put forward in 1880, it was de Mortillet who warned colleagues that this was a devious plot by anti-evolutionist Jesuits to discredit prehistory. This not only led to the cave's contemptuous rejection and a twenty-year delay in the acceptance of cave art, but also was a major cause in the premature death of Sanz de Sautuola, the Spanish landowner who made the claims for Altamira and who, to his horror, was dismissed as naïve or a fraud.

A second major error that arose from de Mortillet's anti-clericalism occurred ten years after his death in 1898. In 1908 the famous Neanderthal skeleton of La Chapelle-aux-Saints was found in France by three priests. Rather than send it for study to the anticlerical École d'Anthropologie, founded by de Mortillet, they entrusted it to the laboratory of Marcellin Boule, a decision which had the gravest consequences for our view of Neanderthals. Boule was greatly influenced by the views of Albert Gaudry, his own teacher, patron, and friend, who did not believe that Neanderthals could be ancestral to modern humans; and so, although aware that the La Chapelle skeleton was an old man whose spine displayed evidence of osteoarthritis, Boule nevertheless claimed that the remains proved Neanderthals could not walk fully erect but were shambling, stooping creatures. Thanks to his overwhelming dominance in the field, the skeleton was not re-examined in detail until the 1950s, and his reconstruction was thought to be so definitive that many other Neanderthal remains were not even reconstructed or reported in any detail, an illustration of the dangers of excessive reliance on the opinions of influential individuals – an understandable but irritating tendency in all aspects of the subject, even today.

So once again a fixed idea about the human past – in this case, that Neanderthals were subhuman brutes – can be traced back to the interaction of personal alliances and antagonisms. Research, and the interpretation and presentation of the past, are inseparable from their social background and the cast of players. One always needs to bear in mind where scholars are 'coming from' and where they are trying to 'get to' in their work and their careers, in order fully to understand the kind of 'accepted fiction' they choose to produce about the past.

But who, then, defines the past that is presented to the public? In Europe's older museums, nineteenth-century views and interpretations still persist in many displays, while most archaeological displays in China remain firmly based on the writings of Marx and Engels. But much effort has been made in recent years, at least in the West, to root out the worst colonialist, racist, and sexist preconceptions. Artefacts are more often presented not in isolation, as works of art, but in their historical context, or in didactic displays showing their function. Museum studies, over the past twenty years, have become an important discipline in their own right, and the complexity of the issues involved in selecting and displaying material to the public has become very apparent.

A fine balance needs to be struck between instructing and entertaining; the dusty, deadly dull museum displays of yesteryear badly needed replacing, but the other extreme needs to be avoided – that of simplistic, sanitized, theme-park versions of the past. The vast majority of archaeological writing still consists of dry tomes, filled with jargon and hot air, and aimed at other scholars; but there is an ever-growing need for what has been called '*haute vulgarisation*' or well-informed popularization, i.e. accessible and readable syntheses that will appeal to the layperson or beginner without loss of content or accuracy. Such books look deceptively simple, but are in fact extremely difficult to pull off, I'm delighted to say – otherwise I would be out of a job. Alas, the more gullible members of the public (and they seem very numerous, judging from sales) constantly fall prey to misguided or downright fraudulent books which spin them ridiculous yarns about ancient astronauts, lost super-civilizations, and so forth.

Other media are also becoming increasingly involved in the exercise. Many countries in Europe, as well as the USA, produce outstanding glossy colour magazines for the public (but still of use to students and specialists) which are devoted to global archaeology. For some reason, Britain – despite massive public interest in the subject – has never managed to produce a successful journal of this kind, and currently has only two magazines devoted to British archaeology and, unfortunately, another aimed specifically at antiquities dealers.

Television and video productions have also become a major vehicle for presenting the past to the public, and consistently achieve high viewing figures, even when the programmes are terrible. The best programmes are those which not only transport the viewing public to places which they may never be able to afford to see, or to which they can never have access, but also present the evidence in a balanced and sober-but-enthusiastic way, avoiding gimmicks and the reckless promotion of sensationalist theories.

Excavators often regard members of the public as a hindrance to their work, but the cannier ones realize the potential financial and other perks to be gained from encouraging the interest of the man in the street. So they organize open days, information sheets, media coverage where possible, and sometimes even fee-paying tours. In Japan, on-the-spot presentations are given as soon as a dig is finished, and details are given to the press the day before, so that the public can read about it in the local morning paper before attending the presentation – as they always do in droves.

There is clearly an avid public appetite for archaeology, which has been a form of entertainment since the early digging of burial mounds (Chapter 1) and the public unwrapping of Egyptian mummies in the last century. The entertainment now has a more scientific and educational form and purpose, but still has to compete with rival popular attractions if archaeology is to thrive or even survive – if public funding were to dry up, so would most archaeology.

We are now in the age of mass tourism and the 'Heritage Industry', and

PUBLIC MUMMY UNWRAPPING TODAY!
STREET URCHIN REQUIRED!

the site often presented as the epitome of how to entertain and instruct the public is the Jorvik Centre in York, northern England. Here, the excavators not only encouraged visits from the public during work on the Viking remains in the late 1970s (a total of half a million visitors over five years), but went on to reconstruct part of the site, complete with streets and houses as the heart of a new museum which is one of the most popular and financially successful to have been created on an archaeological site anywhere in the world. The Centre is located beneath a modern shopping complex. Electronic cars take visitors 'back in time' past thatched houses, workshops, and ships. In and around these structures are lifesize, fibre-glass figures of people in Viking period costume, while a soundtrack provides the noisy atmosphere of a busy street, with adults and children speaking authentic Old Norse, and even appropriate smells have been included, such as around the pigsties and latrine (especially popular with young visitors, as are the scratch-and-sniff postcards). The cars then pass through a simulation of the excavation, and the visitors reach the finds-display and giftshop via a mock-up of a laboratory showing how artefacts and organic remains are studied.

This Centre therefore plays a very important role in presenting a particular site and period to the public, as well as in explaining the sequence of archaeological discovery and interpretation in an imaginative new way. Financially, the Centre has supported new excavations in York, and its success – with over 8 million visitors in the first ten years since its opening in 1984 – has led to similar displays being created in other British towns and other countries. The French replica of Lascaux Cave (necessary since the original can no longer be subjected to mass tourism), opened in 1983, likewise receives several hundred thousand visitors every year, though here, alas, their hefty entrance fees do not contribute to local archaeological research.

The fundamental dilemma of the Heritage Industry is how to balance the paramount requirements of conservation with the public's basic right to see and visit its own patrimony – in other words, how to gauge the known or potential effects of mass tourism on archaeological sites. As archaeology has grown more popular, in tandem with the advent of easy air travel, so a number of towns, regions, and even whole countries – such as China, Peru, Mexico, or Egypt – have become very heavily dependent on archaeological tourism. According to the United Nations, tourism will be the most important activity in the world by the year 2000: it already accounts for 6 per cent of all jobs. This trend is healthy in some respects, since public awareness and enjoyment of archaeology are crucial to the discipline's survival and development in these times of financial stringency, but there are unfortunate consequences. Above all the risks of damage and deterioration, as mentioned earlier; but also the fact that the sites and even the tourists themselves can become targets for terrorism, as has occurred in highland Peru and the Nile Valley: it has proved easy to scare away huge numbers of tourists in this way, and hence – with little effort – have a major impact on the country's economy. For example, by 1995 attacks by Islamic Fundamentalists had cost the Egyptian government at least $2 billion in lost tourist revenues, one of the main sources of hard currency for the country's ailing economy; while the massacre of 58 tourists in Luxor in 1997 has already lost Egypt a further $700 million. Politics can be a thoroughly unpleasant bedfellow for archaeology, as was seen so clearly in the misuses of archaeology by Stalinist Russia and Hitler's Germany.

However politics in archaeology can occasionally be a gentlemanly affair. For example, Charles McBurney, who taught the palaeolithic period at Cambridge University, used to relate how, as an officer during the last war, he had ordered his men to set up camp by a wadi in North Africa – a wadi he had selected because of its Pleistocene terraces. While the men were working, he set off along these terraces, searching for palaeolithic tools. After a while he looked up and noticed that, on the terraces at the other side of the wadi, there was a German officer doing the same thing! 'So we waved to each other, and carried awn!'

The fact is that modern archaeology, as we have seen throughout this book, has many facets and plays many roles; but it can be manipulated by an unscrupulous few for their own ends, as well as by the majority of *bona fide* scholars who wish merely to investigate the past and convey information to a willing public. It only remains, therefore, to look ahead and speculate about the archaeology of tomorrow.

Chapter 10
The Future of the Past

> Historians are left forever chasing shadows, painfully aware of their inability to reconstruct a dead world in its completeness.
>
> (Simon Schama)

Although archaeology is 'a thing of the past', it is still a very young discipline, many of whose basic techniques and theories are recent developments, and as it grows and matures it will certainly continue to flourish and change. In part this will be due to new and major discoveries: not only the spectacular ones which appeal to the tabloids, but also the more modest contributions to our view of the past, such as an earlier date for an event or a cultural phenomenon. The 'joy of archaeology' and its excitement come from these new advances, as well as from the treasures and information aready accumulated, coupled with the knowledge that our picture of the past is constantly changing and will never be finished. For example, the best book synthesizing information on Australian prehistory, Josephine Flood's *Archaeology of the Dreamtime*, has had three editions in only 12 years, and the latest one bears little resemblance to the first, so great and fast are the changes in our knowledge of that country's prehistory. Other topics, such as the origins of humans, or simply of modern humans, are changing so fast that books are out of date before they are published.

It is likely that most of the big discoveries of the future will come from chance finds like the Iceman or the Chauvet Cave, because there will almost certainly be a steady decline in research excavations (as opposed to 'rescue' or 'salvage' excavations which will go on increasing with the growing pace of road construction and urban development). This is partly because new techniques as yet unimagined will increase our ability to 'see' beneath the ground without having to remove it (this is useful since it is the removing of it, by careful, painstaking excavation, which is so very expensive in time and funds); partly through the need to study the immense backlog of excavated material that remains unanalysed and unpublished around the world, causing our museum store-rooms to burst at the seams, or the need to ask new questions of already studied material; and partly because of the growing and urgent need to conserve what we already have, rather than uncover more sites that remain safe beneath the earth.

Indeed conservation will become one of the major foci of the whole subject, as we try to preserve the vast quantities of sites, structures and artefacts, and the millions of known rock art images in the world. Many of the most famous sites are already under tremendous threat – the Sphinx from climatic extremes as well as seepage of sewage water from nearby slums; Tutankhamun's tomb from cracking and the damage caused by floods in 1994; Mohenjodaro, in Pakistan, from erosion and salt corrosion; the Acropolis in Athens from pollution and from climatic change which has caused a black fungus to grow deep within the marble; and the Roman aqueduct in Segovia, Spain, from car pollution, harsh weather and even swift droppings! Dedicated teams from The Getty Conservation Institute of California, or the World Monuments Fund, are making tremendous efforts to preserve and consolidate sites and monuments from all periods and all parts of the world, but even the Getty's apparently limitless resources are but a drop in the ocean when one considers the vast amount of money required to save everything. Hard choices will therefore have to be made (not only in choosing which things to conserve, but in deciding whether to give the money to archaeology at all, rather than to what, in some people's eyes, may be far more deserving or urgent causes) and major efforts continued to record the more vulnerable items such as rock art, inscriptions, and so forth.

At the same time, new technology will come to play an increasingly important role: for example, in the recording of rock art, video cameras and computer enhancement are coming into frequent use, images will be stored using digitization, and the use of a new standardized scale (issued by IFRAO, the International Federation of Rock Art Organizations), which combines measurements with some basic colours, will enable the precise original colours of photographs to be reconstructed by computers in the future, long after the slides or negatives have faded, as they all will. This is a different kind of conservation.

However, the major threats to archaeological sites and material come not so much from natural deterioration or neglect but from damage wrought by humans in a variety of ways. As we have already seen (p. 93), the constantly growing popularity of archaeology also has negative consequences, and mass tourism brings the risk of 'loving archaeology to death' as increasing damage is caused to sites by millions of feet or lungs, quite apart from the (mercifully far rarer) damage caused deliberately by vandals or, less purposefully, by warfare or wargames: for instance, the military have done great damage during exercises on Salisbury Plain and in southern France. As the threat of a Cold War recedes, they unleash their tanks and firepower on prehistoric burial mounds.

But there is another, far more destructive factor, which has been with us for millennia (e.g. the tomb-robbers of ancient Egypt, p. 80) but which has exploded in recent years – the looting of archaeological sites by those who dig for monetary gain, searching only for saleable objects and generally destroying everything else. Warfare can help them enormously, as for instance in Lebanon, where the hostilities led to the mass looting of the country's antiquities, and thousands of tons of artefacts were secretly

shipped out by militiamen and unscrupulous dealers. The great structures of Angkor Wat in Cambodia deteriorated rapidly during the conflicts there, owing to the prolonged interruption of maintenance, but also to massive looting during Pol Pot's regime. Afghanistan's national archaeological museum, outside Kabul, is still being repeatedly shelled and ransacked as factions fight it out in that country.

The saddest aspect of this looting is the loss of information when finds are cut off from their original context. The objects may be beautiful in our eyes, but the information they could have provided is incalculable. It is like the difference between seeing captionless photographs of unknown people from the last century, and seeing pictures with full explanatory texts regarding date, subject matter, and so forth. The former may be occasionally striking, or pretty, or interesting (e.g. for the fashions being worn), but one gets infinitely more from the captioned images. This is what the collectors of antiquities fail to grasp – they know the price of everything and the value of nothing.

It is certainly modern collectors who are the true villains of the piece. One cannot really blame impoverished peasants in the Third World for seeking 'valuable' objects in the ground, knowing that they can earn more to feed their families from selling one good find than from a year of hard work. But in other countries such as Britain and America there are well-organized professional gangs of looters, who are not only equipped with hi-tech gadgets, but also well armed. If there was no ready market, if the doors were effectively closed – as they were for the ivory trade a few years ago – then prices would fall, markets would disappear, and the trade might decline. As it is, however, it is booming, despite stringent laws applied by some countries. In China, for example, thieves can be executed for looting ancient tombs and smuggling antiquities out of the country, yet vast quantities of material are haemorrhaging into Hong Kong at a rapidly accelerating rate and from there to collectors around the world: for example, thieves ransacked 40,000 ancient tombs in China in 1989 and 1990 alone; and in the first half of 1994, customs officials seized $5.5 million worth of smuggled artefacts in Hong Kong, four times the total for the whole of 1993, and yet only a tiny fraction of the loot is being intercepted. In 1997, Chinese customs seized more than 11,200 smuggled antiquities, and about 6,000 in the first half of 1998; conversely, in 1998 3,000 antiquities discovered by British customs in 1994 were returned to China.

It has been said, quite correctly, that 'collectors are the real looters'. Many collectors try to justify their activities by claiming that, without them, all these beautiful *objets d'art* would not be preserved, and that museums do not have the resources to look after their collections properly. There is some truth in both these views, but it is outweighed by the ugly little fact that it is the market and the astronomical prices paid for objects to decorate Swiss apartments or Manhattan mantelpieces which ultimately feed the looting monster, and which cause tens of thousands of ancient tombs and other sites to be ransacked and annihilated every year. Even museums are being plundered now, with objects that are published (and could never be put on open sale) being stolen apparently to order – presumably for some sad, selfish, crackpot megalomaniac to gloat over in private, as he or she strokes a white cat and dreams of dominating the world, or perhaps of getting a life.

The brighter and more democratic side of archaeology's popularity' is the blossoming of heritage centres and museums around the world, with interactive computer terminals; ultramodern displays that are striking and didactic and fun; places where one can do some kind of experimental archaeology; and even 'hands-on discovery centres', offering 'a chance to meet an archaeologist' (don't all rush at once). Holograms are already appearing in the wealthier museums, and virtual-reality technology is being developed that enables people to visit sites that no longer exist (such as the medieval French abbey of Cluny) or that cannot be opened to mass tourism (such as the Ice Age decorated caves of Lascaux and Cosquer). Eventually, therefore, a great deal of archaeological tourism will be done at home, from an armchair, and this will relieve the pressure on sites, although increasing tourism and the ever-broadening horizons of tourists are always putting pressure on new areas.

All of these things are in their infancy, and were unheard of just a decade or two ago, so in view of the extreme acceleration of this new technology it is impossible to imagine what the future will hold for archaeology in this domain, or in those of new dating methods, or satellite reconnaissance, or in genetic clues to the origins and development of humans and their domestic plants and animals. There will certainly be even more reliance on the expertise of boffins. It is a fair

bet that the trend of doing more with less (p. 12) will go on, while there will probably be a growing emphasis on historical archaeology in countries where the indigenous communities object to, or need to be consulted about, new fieldwork on prehistoric material (this has already happened in Australia and elsewhere).

What we can say with some certainty is that the archaeology of the future will be more anonymous, continuing the trend away from big personalities and 'characters' that we have already seen through this century. The navel-gazing will undoubtedly continue, amid the growing awareness of the weakness of our basic assumptions, and of the fact that other groups of people also have claims on the remains of the past – the militant actions of some minorities (Chapter 8) will spread rapidly to other parts of the world such as South America and Africa.

Yet archaeology, as long as it can go on 'delivering the goods' and hence earning its public funding and support, will continue to flourish, because it remains the *only* subject that can study 99 per cent of the human past. Only archaeology can tell us about the really fundamental events in our past – when, where, and how humankind arose in the first place; the development of art, of technology, of writing; the origins and spread of agriculture, of complex societies, of urbanization. These are just a few of the huge variety of topics being actively investigated by researchers all over the world, and much remains to be done in every domain, to fit more pieces into the vast jigsaw puzzle of the human record. With its uniquely long-term view archaeology is our only means of seeing the 'big picture'. If we want to know where we're going, we need to trace our trajectory, to see where we've come from. That is why archaeology is so important.

Further Reading

If you would now like to delve further into the wonderful world of archaeology, here are a few books that should meet your needs and direct you on to a vast library of further reading (especially the references given in Renfrew and Bahn 2000).

AITKEN, M. J. (1990), *Science-based Dating in Archaeology*. Longman: London and New York.

BAHN, P. G. (ed.) (1995), *The Story of Archaeology: 100 Great Discoveries*. Barnes & Noble: New York/ Weidenfeld & Nicolson: London. (Heavily illustrated volume presenting archaeology's 'greatest hits' and something of its amazing diversity and versatility.)

—— (ed.) (1996), *The Cambridge Illustrated History of Archaeology*. Cambridge University Press: Cambridge. (The history and development of the subject, all over the world.)

—— (1999) *The Bluffer's Guide to Archaeology* (revised edition) Oval Books: London. (A humorous introduction to the subject.)

—— (ed.) (2000), *The Penguin Guide to Archaeology*. Penguin: London.

—— (ed.) (2000), *Atlas of World Archaeology*. Cassell: London.

BARKER, P. (1993), *Techniques of Archaeological Excavation*. (3rd edn.) Batsford: London/Humanities Press: New York. (The best introduction to British excavation methods.)

COLES, J. M. (1979), *Experimental Archaeology*. Academic Press: London and New York.

Courbin, P. (1988), *What is Archaeology? An essay on the nature of archaeological research*. University of Chicago Press: Chicago. (A detailed critique of the 'New Archeology'.)

Dark, K. T. (1995), *Theoretical Archaeology*. Duckworth: London. (A useful student textbook of theory.)

Fagan, B. (1995), *Time Detectives: How archaeologists use technology to recapture the past*, Simon & Schuster: New York. (Case-studies showing the variety and scope of modern archaeology.)

—— (ed.) (1996), *The Oxford Companion to Archaeology*. Oxford University Press: New York.

Green, E. L. (ed.) (1984), *Ethics and Values in Archaeology*. Free Press: New York.

McIntosh, J. (1999), *The Archaeologist's Handbook*. (2nd edn.) Thames and Hudson: London.

Parkes, P. A. (1986), *Current Scientific Techniques in Archaeology*. Croom Helm: London and Sydney.

Purdy, B. A. (1996), *How to do Archaeology the right way*. University Press of Florida: Gainesville. (An American approach to excavation.)

Renfrew, C. and Bahn, P. G. (2000), *Archaeology: Theories, Methods and Practice*. (3rd edn.) Thames and Hudson: London and New York. (A brick-like textbook covering all the major aspects of the subject, including everything in this book, in great but readable detail.)

Index

CLASSICS

A Very Short Introduction

Mary Beard and John Henderson

This Very Short Introduction to Classics links a haunting temple on a lonely mountainside to the glory of ancient Greece and the grandeur of Rome, and to Classics within modern culture – from Jefferson and Byron to Asterix and Ben-Hur.

> 'The authors show us that Classics is a "modern" and sexy subject. They succeed brilliantly in this regard ... nobody could fail to be informed and entertained – and the accent of the book is provocative and stimulating.'
>
> **John Godwin, *Times Literary Supplement***

> 'Statues and slavery, temples and tragedies, museum, marbles, and mythology – this provocative guide to the Classics demysties its varied subject-matter while seducing the reader with the obvious enthusiasm and pleasure which mark its writing.'
>
> **Edith Hall**

MUSIC

A Very Short Introduction

Nicholas Cook

This stimulating Very Short Introduction to music invites us to really *think* about music and the values and qualities we ascribe to it.

'A *tour de force*. Nicholas Cook is without doubt one of the most probing and creative thinkers about music we have today.'

Jim Samson, University of Bristol

'Nicholas Cook offers a perspective that is clearly influenced by recent writing in a host of disciplines related to music. It may well prove a landmark in the appreciation of the topic ... In short, I can hardly imagine it being done better.'

Roger Parker, University of Cambridge

www.oup.co.uk/vsi/music